Brilliant Ideas for Using ICT in the Inclusive Classroom

How can you use ICT to boost the achievement of *all* your pupils?

This practical teachers' guide will help you to unlock the enormous potential of new technology in order to enhance pupils' learning, particularly for young people with additional needs. Written by two of the UK's leading technology experts, this invaluable new resource will enable you to use ICT effectively to make lessons more accessible, motivating and fun.

With 50 illustrated case studies and 20 starter activities, this practical resource will help you to introduce new technology into the inclusive classroom. It has been specifically designed to help develop your pupils' key skills, such as problem solving, developing concepts and communicating to different audiences. In each activity, the authors show why and how a particular resource was used and show how similar techniques can be implemented to open up the curriculum to *your* learners.

The authors include timely and realistic advice on how to use a range of technologies from the cheap and cheerful – and even free – to more sophisticated and specialist packages. Find out about:

- podcasting
- digital animation
- iPods and iPads
- dance mat technology
- digital storytelling
- wikis
- online reading schemes

- sat nav
- storyboarding
- games and gaming
- mobile phones
- art packages
- using sound
- visualisers

Whether you're already techno-savvy or looking to get started with ICT, this book is full of brilliant ideas on how to engage learners of all abilities using technology. If you're looking for inspiration on how to integrate creative uses of ICT with the curriculum, this book will prove invaluable.

Sally McKeown is an award-winning journalist who specialises in disability. She has taught in schools and colleges, supporting students with a wide range of learning needs, and now runs training courses for charities and educators.

Angela McGlashon is a former teacher, Senior Lecturer at Anglia Ruskin University and the University of Essex, Local Authority adviser, business manager and trainer for a variety of software companies. She is now a freelance consultant working with many mainstream and special schools.

Other titles published in association with the National Association for Special Educational Needs (nasen):

Forthcoming titles:

Language for Learning in the Secondary School: A Practical Guide for Supporting Students with Speech, Language and Communication Needs
Sue Hayden and Emma Jordan
2012/pb: 978-0-415-61975-2

ADHD: All Your Questions Answered: A Complete Handbook for SENCOs and Teachers
Fintan O'Regan
2012/pb: 978-0-415-59770-8

Assessing Children with Specific Learning Difficulties: A Teacher's Practical Guide
Gavin Reid, Gad Elbeheri and John Everatt
2012/pb: 978-0-415-67027-2

Using Playful Practice to Communicate with Special Children
Margaret Corke
2012/pb: 978-0-415-68767-6

The Equality Act for Educational Professionals: A simple guide to disability and inclusion in schools
Geraldine Hills
2012/pb: 978-0-415-68768-3

More Trouble with Maths: A teacher's complete guide to identifying and diagnosing mathematical difficulties
Steve Chinn
2012/pb: 978-0-415-67013-5

Dyslexia and Inclusion: Classroom Approaches for Assessment, Teaching and Learning
Gavin Reid
2012/pb: 978-0-415-60758-2

Available now:

Brilliant Ideas for Using ICT in the Inclusive Classroom
Sally McKeown and Angela McGlashon
2011/pb: 978-0-415-67254-2

The SENCO Survival Guide: The Nuts and Bolts of Everything You Need to Know
Sylvia Edwards
2010/pb:978-0-415-59281-9

The SEN Handbook for Trainee Teachers, NQTs and Teaching Assistants
Wendy Spooner
2010/pb:978-0-415-56771-8

Attention Deficit Hyperactivity Disorder: What Can Teachers Do?
Geoff Kewley
2010/pb:978-0-415-49202-7

Young People with Anti-Social Behaviours: Practical Resources for Professionals
Kathy Hampson
2010/pb: 978-0-415-56570-7

Confronting Obstacles to Inclusion: International responses to developing inclusive education
Richard Rose
2010/pb:978-0-415-49363-5

Supporting Children's Reading: A Complete Short Course for Teaching Assistants, Volunteer Helpers and Parents
Margaret Hughes and Peter Guppy
2010/pb: 978-0-415-49836-4

Dyspraxia 5-14: Identifying and Supporting Young People with Movement Difficulties
Christine Macintyre
2009/pb: 978-0-415-54396-5

A Handbook for Inclusion Managers: Steering your School towards Inclusion
Ann Sydney
2009/pb: 978-0-415-49198-3

Living With Dyslexia: The social and emotional consequences of specific learning difficulties/disabilities
Barbara Riddick and Angela Fawcett
2009/pb: 978-0-415-47758-1

Brilliant Ideas for Using ICT in the Inclusive Classroom

Sally McKeown and
Angela McGlashon

Routledge
Taylor & Francis Group

LONDON AND NEW YORK

Helping Everyone Achieve

First published 2012
by Routledge
2 Park Square, Milton Park, Abingdon, Oxon OX14 4RN

Simultaneously published in the USA and Canada
by Routledge
711 Third Avenue, New York, NY 10017

Routledge is an imprint of the Taylor & Francis Group, an informa business

British Library Cataloguing in Publication Data
A catalogue record for this book is available from the British Library

Library of Congress Cataloging in Publication Data
McKeown, Sally.
Brilliant ideas for using ICT in the inclusive classroom / Sally McKeown and Angela McGlashon.
p. cm.
1. Educational technology. 2. Information technology--Study and teaching. 3. Inclusive education. I. McGlashon, Angela. II. Title.
LB1028.3.M398 2011
371.33--dc22
2011013708

ISBN: 978-0-415-67254-2 (pbk)
ISBN: 978-0-203-80256-4 (ebk)

Typeset in Times New Roman
by Saxon Graphics Ltd, Derby

MIX
Paper from
responsible sources
FSC® C004839

Printed and bound in Great Britain by the MPG Books Group

nasen is a professional membership association that supports all those who work with or care for children and young people with special and additional educational needs. Members include teachers, teaching assistants, support workers, other educationalists, students and parents.

nasen supports its members through policy documents, journals, its magazine Special!, publications, professional development courses, regional networks and newsletters. Its website contains more current information such as responses to government consultations. **nasen's** published documents are held in very high regard both in the UK and internationally.

CONTENTS

Acknowledgements

Many people contributed to this book. Particular thanks are due to Dr Linda Evans, Editor of *SENCO Update*, who suggested the original idea and Daniel McKeown for first line editing and research.

Thanks also to: Louise Wharton – Stanley School Wirral; Jack Todhunter – Newman School Rotherham; Mark Slawinski – Culture24; Michael Leeming – Storrington & District Museum Society; Lindsay Nadin – Pearson; Steve Harris – Richard Lander School Cornwall; Ann Crick, Moira Turton – West Oaks School & Technology College Boston Spa; staff at plasq.com; Peter Everett – Whitmore Junior School Basildon; staff and pupils at Grangehurst School Coventry; Rob Laird – Streetley Sports College; Tamworth School Sport Partnership; Brendan Routledge – Suffolk Education Consultants; Diane Hasell – The Bridge at Hadley Learning Community in Telford; Pravin Jethwa – AmazingInteractives; anna Hughes – The Nuneaton Academy; Tim James – Caludon Castle School Coventry; National Association for Teaching English (NATE); Nick Day – Orwell High School in Felixstowe; Sean O'Sullivan – Frank Wise School in Banbury; Rebecca Cole – Glenaire Primary School in Shipley; Rosie Murphy – Fairfield School in Batley; Alison Littlewood – Inclusive Technology; Sarah Clark and Lynn O'Brien – Isobel Mair School in East Renfrewshire; staff and pupils Dorin Park School in Cheshire; Cheryl Dobbs – Independent Education Consultant, Gillian Penny; Gavinburn Primary School West Dunbartonshire; James Betts Kudlian software; staff and pupils at Tennyson Road Primary School in Luton; Gemma Holmes – 2Simple; Bev Evans Pembroke Dock Community School; Andrea Carr – Rising Stars; Jenny Langley – the Manchester Academy; Rachel Tomlin –Heathermount School in Berkshire; Donna Burton-Wilcock – Immersive Education; Simon Fitzpatrick – Independent Consultant; Sandra Miller – FACCT in Fife; Pauline Winter – Clapham Terrace Primary in Warwickshire; Alison Carter Longwill School for Deaf Children in Birmingham; K.C.Kelly-Markwick – Oakwood Court College in Devon; Danny Nicolson, ICT Consultant Southend; Helen Davis – Davison C of E High School for Girls in Worthing; Birmingham School Effectiveness Division; Birmingham Library Services; Maggie Wagstaff Independent Consultant; Alex Jones – Sheffield West City Learning Centre Andrea Keightley – Montsaye Community College in Northamptonshire; Stuart Porter – TrueTube; Carol Allen, advisory teacher for ICT and special needs in North Tyneside; Dawn Hallybone and Alissa Chesters – Oakdale Junior School in the London Borough of Redbridge; Debbie La – Montrose Road Centre Forfar; Dr Benjaman Schogler-Skoogmusic Limited; Mandy Nelms – Priorslee Primary School in Telford; staff and pupils at St. Matthews Academy in Lewisham; David Vernon – Broadgreen Primary School in Liverpool; Janice Wilson – Astley Park School in Chorley; Yvonne Aylott – Westfield Technology College in Weymouth; staff and pupils at The Old Railway School in Ashford, Kent; Anna James – Access Through Technology Co-ordinator Norfolk; Sarah Melton The Clare School in Norwich; staff and pupils at Brentwood Special School in Altrincham Cheshire; Gareth Morewood – Priestnall School, Stockport; Heather Truelove Tameside MBC; Sue Stevens – Royal School for the Deaf in Derby; Nathan Cresswell – Pioneer School Essex Cuckmere House School – Seaford, East Sussex; madeinme; Lorraine Petersen NASEN; staff at Livewire PR; staff at Mango Marketing.

Foreword

ICT in education: the road ahead

Ray Barker

It was Lord Stevenson in 1997 who really started the ICT revolution in schools by telling Tony Blair that if his new government wanted to make a difference to twenty-first-century education, he would have to make 'a leap of faith': take ICT seriously and invest in a big way. And that is exactly what happened: first came an emphasis on infrastructure, then on connectivity and training and finally on digital content. The result, although we sometimes forget it, is the development of ICT in education that is the envy of the world.

Of course we realised very early that the investment in 'stuff' does not make the difference; it is the teaching profession that mediates technology as a tool to make a difference to what happens in classrooms.

We learned through our own mistakes that ICT was not the only way of dealing with teaching; that it was a perfect solution to a specific problem – not a panacea for all children, classrooms, and teachers. You have a problem? What's the best solution? It may be glue and glitter, it may be iPads or it may be data loggers.

The big issue, and the great change for education, has come with the focus on objectives and outcomes. What needs to be achieved and what are the best tools to achieve this? Is technology appropriate? With the growth in the 'personalised learning' movement, dealing with learning styles and the impact of any learning

space or environment, what is suitable may be a mixture of resources – technology being only one and being used by only a few. It's actually about 'micro' level thinking in classes – not 'macro'.

It is interesting to reflect on research I was involved in as far back as 2000. This aimed to find common characteristics of effective ICT use. The first was that increased practice is a key feature of how ICT can help improve learning. Computers can motivate young people to undertake such practice and make sure that they are doing so at an appropriate level. The second was that feedback provided by ICT – often immediate – can help children learn in a variety of ways. The third was that ICT is powerful in presenting or representing information in a variety of ways – and that this can be adapted or changed quickly. Lastly we found that ICT could help to develop pupils' thinking in a range of ways including reasoning, understanding and creativity. We may be close to 12 years on now, but these themes still recur in the case studies in this book. The big difference is that now we know that effective use also depends on the choices that a teacher makes about how to use ICT as a part of their teaching.

This has big implications for the sustainability of effective ICT use in schools. First is the need for training and CPD as ICT becomes more sophisticated and pedagogies change. Often such support was provided by government agencies or Local Authorities. Recent announcements on funding have either scrapped such agencies or will lead to a decline in LA personnel. Education institutions will have to find a way of securing training, or at least time to allow educators to 'play' with ICT in order to see what it can do specifically for them in their day-to-day work. Industry, those suppliers of equipment and digital content, will step in to fill this gap. They need the support of educators to keep the momentum of technology. The challenge will be from the schools themselves and whether there will be the time (this means money) or even the will to make this happen if ICT is not a core subject or if Ofsted does not look closely at provision and implementation.

The second big issue is raising the awareness of teachers about what is 'out there'. They can look in catalogues, talk to others or even visit BETT, but even after this how are they able to make the right choices? This book and its case studies will make a vital contribution to this cause. The chapters show exactly what was used, why and how – and the results. It's therefore practical and realistic; it talks in the right language.

So, we are entering a time of change. The focus on ICT from government has diminished, as have the ring-fenced grants to ensure infrastructure and use. We need to keep this momentum going. This book is therefore very timely: it is full of practical examples rooted in real practice – just what educators need. The resources and solutions range from the often cheap – and even free – to the most specialist. Even better, it contains help-sheets so you can get on and try things out in your classroom.

This book shows what can be done with ICT and the positive effects achieved; the most powerful influence is going to be teachers 'talking' to teachers. Young people now have very high expectations of technology. Who are we to disappoint them?

Ray Barker is director of BESA (British Educational Suppliers Association).

Part 1

Brilliant Ideas

Brilliant Idea 1

Getting smart with the versatile SmartBoard

PEOPLE OFTEN THINK interactive whiteboards are a front-of-the-class presentation tool, but at Stanley School on the Wirral, a special school for pupils with complex learning difficulties, they really come into their own when used with individual children. A mixture of visuals, sound and well chosen activities can stimulate the most reluctant learners.

Louise Wharton is a Learning Support Assistant at the school and works with Year 6. The nine children in her class include one child with Down's Syndrome, some with ASD and a number who have complex communication difficulties. The school was just getting SmartBoards when she joined four years ago. She was quite confident about 'having a go' on the computer and quickly realised there were lots of things she could make and adapt to attract the children's attention and help their focus.

'We use the SmartBoard in so many ways. We start in the morning using them for registration. The children touch their name or their picture. They can copy over their name with a pen to practise the letter shapes. We have created some "magic paper". Their name is hidden on the board but it is written in the same colour as the background so it is invisible until they drag a square of a different colour over it. Then their name magically appears and they can look and see how it is spelt and have another go. We also use our SmartBoard for the timetable. We use Communicate in Print Symbols and each day is colour coded too.

'When I arrived at the school I started seeing what we could do at lunchtime. I did some drawings and used the scenes on the Smart Notebook software: some children liked football so I made a football scene for them. One child is mad about animals so I got animal sounds on the board for him. Cars are popular too so I put up different colours and models of cars; again, I attached sound files so when the children pressed a picture, they got a noise. All the children I am working with now can walk up to the board and touch it and they like the interaction: they touch it and something happens.

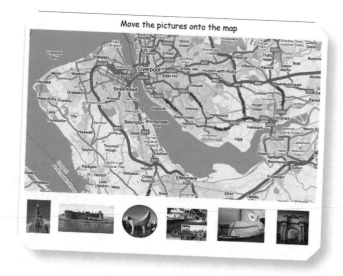

Move the pictures onto the map

'But it wasn't always the case: when we first started with the SmartBoard, it was new and different. While some children loved it, others didn't want to go near it, so we had to find a hook to lure them in. One of my little girls didn't respond positively to anything we were doing but I knew she loved babies so I took the sound of a baby crying and attached it to a picture of a dolly and she went up and touched the whiteboard. It was a very small achievement but it was nice she cooperated and enjoyed what she was doing.

'What I really like about Smart Notebook software is it is so easy to adapt things. Often software is not very flexible and we need to change things to get the maximum response so the children can show they are interested and participate. We use it for matching activities with symbols. We usually attach a sound clip to the symbol for extra reinforcement and to give them a response. We use the Oxford Reading Tree scheme and some children prefer the digital version to the book. It seems to keep them focused for longer and they sometimes make more progress.

'We also use it in maths for simple adding, matching blocks and numbers. One of the little boys loved drums so I made an activity where he has had to drag five drums to match the number 5. With the sound effects it was quite noisy! For science we did some sorting activities. I made two pages, one for a forest and one

You could ...

✔ Make drag-and-drop sorting activities

✔ Use the creative pens to write their names

✔ Use a thick white pen to draw over pictures so that the screen appears totally white until they start to rub out using the eraser! Great for a bug hunt!

✔ By sending some images and words to the back layer, make a picnic basket that only takes healthy food (the other foods are left on the top layer!)

✔ Make a puppet theatre with a background and people to move on top. If you choose 'recorder' from the task bar pop-up icon you can record the action with sound

✔ Create visual timetables, star charts and certificates easily and quickly

✔ Link sounds, videos and other pages to objects so children can choose how to 'read' the story

✔ Use the infinite cloner to make a limitless supply of coins, shapes, words or images for tessellation, ordering, sequencing or calculations

✔ Take snap shots of videos to use as a storyboard (use the camera tool)

for a pond. Along the bottom of the page were pictures of creatures and the children had to drag them onto the appropriate page.

'I made some pages about the decades 1930-1960 for a complex communication group. We decided the best way to approach the topic was to give them a taste of the times so I had six pictures on each page and included a phone, car, dress, and washing machine for each period and a couple of other things. When they touched the screen, they got some music from the decade. It is quite important to have some consistency for our learners so if the pages for a topic have a similar format they know what they are looking at and don't get confused. Once you have your basic layout, you can adapt it if it does not work for an individual child.'

Contacts and information

http://www.teachingideas.co.uk/

Brilliant Idea 2

Disney and Spielberg need to look to their laurels

NEWMAN SCHOOL IN Rotherham is a Specialist School for Cognition & Learning. A few years ago Jack Todhunter, teacher of English at the school, started to use Apple technology with the program I Can Animate. Since then, the school has won a number of awards for its work with claymation and digital animation.

'*Theseus and the Minor Detour* was one of our first attempts,' said Jack, 'and although we have moved on, we are still very fond of it. We were amused when someone at Cambridge University cited it as a good example of getting children to engage with the classics! So far as they were concerned it was just a good story and fun to animate.'

'I always feel we should encourage "stealth reading" where pupils engage with a variety of texts but don't realise how hard they are working,' said Jack. At the moment we are animating the witches scene in *Macbeth* and in the past we have worked on *King Lear*, *Othello*, *Wuthering Heights*, *Great Expectations* – not many mainstream schools could claim as much.'

Newman School had two entries in the recent National Schools Film and Animation Awards run by TAG Learning Limited. *Homage to Hitch* features a strange bird which 'haunts' a couple of villagers and was the culmination of work on Daphne Du Maurier and Alfred Hitchcock. The storyboard itself emanated from a genuine article in *The Daily Mail* which, by happy coincidence, was published in the middle of the project. As preparation for the piece, the students had to ground themselves in a number of genres including short story, film and journalism before turning their hand to animation. The result is a story full of suspense and humour. Their second piece was *Safety*

on the Internet which combines drawings, computer graphics, avatars and synthetic speech to create a short piece with a very futuristic feel.

The whole process is very engaging. Creating the models in clay is quite therapeutic for those children who can be hyperactive and they all really enjoy the 'making' part of the process. 'When we made *Homage to Hitch*, we had several versions of the clay figures which were farmed out around the class. We storyboarded the action and people could choose which parts they wanted to animate and edit. It was a very collaborative approach. After all, at Aardman Animations, the company that produced *Wallace and Gromit*, they have a team of 60 or so animators so we should aim to work in the same way. We also had a parents' evening and let them animate a couple of frames so they got a feeling for the skills involved. Some parents were so taken with the project that they have bought computers and animation software to use at home.'

You could ...

✔ Host inter-school competitions

✔ Use it for after-school clubs

✔ Make it a feature of transition activities where primary and secondary pupils come together

✔ Hold community events

✔ Animate a story, poem or song

✔ Use finger puppets to use as animation characters

✔ Animate inanimate objects such as pens, knives and forks or Lego

✔ Animate a process in history or science such as mummifying in Egypt or birds making a nest

✔ Use a visualiser to animate ice melting, flowers fading or mould growing by utilising the delayed snapshot on the visualiser

✔ Capture the movements of the class pet as it moves around the bowl or cage

Contacts and information

Newman school has used a range of software for their work:
Crazy Talk 6 – http://www.taglearning.com/
I Can Animate – http://www.kudlian.net/
Noodle Flix – http://noodle-flix.en.softonic.com/mac
Xtranormal – http://www.xtranormal.com/
Claymation – http://www.ikitmovie.com/59/claymation.htm

See the videos online at:
Theseus and the Minor Detour
http://www.youtube.com/watch?v=YMPDOcohcLY

Homage to Hitch
http://schoolstube.com/asset/view/id/937/code/1eec34

Brilliant Idea 3

Visit museums online and become a Caboodle curator!

SO MANY ARTEFACTS which represent the nation's heritage are to be found in museums. They give us a unique insight into our past, from the agricultural traditions in Britain to the conditions for slaves coming into Liverpool before heading out to the New World. These days it can be really hard to organise school trips on a regular basis. A project called Caboodle run by Culture24 opens up some of the best museums to children and gives them the chance to develop some curator skills with collections of their own.

Mark Slawinski, Staff Writer and Outreach Co-ordinator at Culture24 explains what Caboodle can offer: 'Caboodle is Culture24's fun, free and safe collections website for children. On it, children become digital curators to exhibit their precious things as well as photos of the world around them. Caboodle is a website which lets young people become digital curators, collecting and exchanging collections of digital photos.

'It is free but you need to sign up to it and then you can submit an endless stream of digital images. These collections could be stickers, Lego, clothing, shells, artwork, bike bits, books or anything which interests you. Caboodle guides offer the following categories: Arty, Nature, People, Random, Toys and Treasures, but users can add their own.'

Some museums are already heavily involved: the Royal Armouries have already Caboodled two sets of outstanding content including Elephant Armour, Henry VIII's 'Horned Helmet' and a mysterious and exotic 'Dasta Bungha' from the sixteenth century. There are many amazing museum objects on the site to inspire children. They may then create a set in response, learn new facts about the nation's treasures or be inspired to start a new collection of their own.

Flower Fairies Fold-out Book
The shape of this is really cool and the pictures are amazing. I'd like to do some drawings like these in Art.
Photo 4 of 5

PREV   NEXT   X CLOSE

Other museums have signed up and opened their doors to the Caboodle project. One of the really exciting aspects of the site is its ability to allow young people to have fun describing collection items on a museum's behalf. Storrington Museum in West Sussex recently let a group of young Caboodlers take photos of their collection, and the resulting Caboodle can be seen in various categories on the site.

Caboodle presents a fun opportunity for museums to 'repackage' a sample from their collections. We've had three great sets from English Heritage, a sample of the Designated Collection from the Horniman Museum along with their must-see giant walrus, and various action-packed Caboodles from the Jorvik Viking Centre and The Shakespeare Birthplace Trust.

You could ...

✔ Link to the local museum and ask them to visit

✔ Find a Caboodle and create activities around it

✔ As a class make a Caboodle and post it online

✔ Run an after-school Curators' Club

✔ Use it as an opportunity for children who are experts on a topic to showcase their knowledge

✔ Using an art package, select, copy and paste part of an exhibit to create a pattern

✔ Put a colour wash over an object

✔ Use special effects to create an impressionist or Pop Art version

✔ Create a museum of your own with labels

✔ Record labels for your museum

✔ Make a photostory (using Photo Story 3 from Microsoft)

✔ Use the images to create sorting activities

✔ Use the images to make a quiz

✔ Make a treasure trail by putting images around for pupils to find

✔ Give some clues for pupils to identify the correct image

✔ Make a 'what could this be used for?' quiz

Contacts and information

http://www.caboodle.org.uk/
http://www.show.me.uk/

Brilliant Idea 4

An online world opens reading to boys

Bug Club

BOYS' LITERACY HAS been a key area of concern for some time. There is a shortage of male role models in primary settings with a preponderance of female teachers, so reading is sometimes seen as something that girls do. But computer reading schemes can seem more real for some children and the virtual book bag is always to hand so the cry of 'I left my book at school' just doesn't cut it.

Bug Club from Pearson features well known characters such as Wallace and Gromit. Children might read the books in print form or go for the online version which they can access on any computer with an internet connection. They can also earn Bug points for completing interactive reading activities and then exchange these points for rewards such as decorating their own tree-house or growing their own dragon. It seems that for some boys the element of competition is very motivating.

Kate Ruttle is SENCO at Great Heath Primary School, Mildenhall, Suffolk where they have trained a teaching assistant in the Fischer Family Trust Wave 3 programme to improve literacy skills.

'Charlie is a very active little boy who has always been unwilling to sit down, to read and to write. Assessments suggest that he has low average receptive vocabulary and a poor short term memory. All of the children in school have daily phonics sessions in attainment sets. Charlie was doing the phase 3 work for the third time because he hadn't made the progress we had hoped. This had previously been put down to his behaviour but it quickly became apparent that part of Charlie's difficulty was that he didn't 'get' the point of phonics.

'By the end of Year 1, he was realising that he was falling behind his peers and his behaviour worsened. This pattern continued at the beginning of Year 2 and we were hesitant about taking him into the programme.

You could ...

✔ Make your own stories from the characters in the books

✔ Use Publisher or 2Simple's 2Publish to make your own short book from the leaflet or flyer template

✔ Make a poster about the sound, book or activity

✔ Get the children to record story tapes for other children to listen to (using Easi-Speak microphones)

However, he was really keen because he liked the idea of reading the Star Wars books or the Wallace and Gromit books.'

For Charlie, the value of Bug Club is twofold: the small steps in the Bug Club let him make progress without fear of failure, and the clusters of books give him incentives to move on. Charlie's behaviour is now much improved and he is generally willing to make an attempt at anything that is offered to him – including writing which was once a significant trigger for temper tantrums. Although he is still working behind the expected level for his age, Charlie is now learning to learn and enjoying becoming a reader.

Contacts and information
Bug Club – http://tinyurl.com/6gkbjss

Brilliant Idea 5

Learning French: quicker with Clicker

LEARNING A FOREIGN language is fun but is challenging too, especially for pupils who might have problems with their own language. In addition, many teachers in primary or special schools are not language specialists and may worry that they are 'doing it wrong'.

Moira Turton at West Oaks Special School has been using Clicker French in regular whole-class sessions with Key Stage 3 and 4 students. All of the students have special needs and approximately a third are diagnosed as having an autistic spectrum disorder. It is very much a mixed ability group: some of the children are at P level, whilst others are up at Level 4 in their speaking and reading.

They have responded particularly well to the 'Jack and the Beanstalk' section of the French Stories CD. First, they looked at the story together as a class. 'The children absolutely loved it; they recognised a lot of the story from the English version they were all so familiar with,' said Moira. The children particularly enjoyed the Raconte l' histoire activity, in which they retold the story by choosing the correct picture to match each statement they were hearing. 'We did this as a whole-class activity, with each child taking one statement so everyone could contribute. There was a real sense of achievement amongst the students when we had completed the whole story'.

The pupils all used microphones to record themselves saying various sentences from the story. Many of the children proved to have good imitative skills and listening to an authentic French voice meant that they made rapid progress in their pronunciation. After a few practices, some were getting it absolutely spot on! 'Hearing the story in French really helped them to understand the meaning of the new words they were introduced to, not to mention how much fun they had in the process! Most of all, I was amazed at the confidence the children developed.

'As the term progressed, they became really comfortable with speaking in French in front of their

classmates and were happy to come up to the front and give all the activities a try. They used to welcome the MFL Advisor by speaking in French whenever she came into the classroom! In fact, when we invited some neighbouring high school students to come and join in with one of our sessions, they were bowled over by how confident and assured my pupils were'.

What a multimedia framework can offer:
1. Encourages pupils to correct pronunciation
2. Provides real models of speech
3. Promotes reading independence with talking books
4. Provides a grid with writing prompts
5. Provides picture support to help with memory
6. Supports pupils with written work

You could ...

✔ Create your own resources using Clicker or similar products

✔ Take photos of pupils and put them in a grid with a sound clip

✔ Put photos of celebrities on a grid and build a vocabulary list of adjectives

✔ List their likes and dislikes: J'adore, no me gusta, etc.

✔ Use symbols to reinforce vocabulary

✔ Get pupils to create or use emoticons for different moods: Je suis heureuse ☺, estoy triste ☹

Contacts and information
Clicker French and Spanish –
  http://www.cricksoft.com

Brilliant Idea 6

Words on the move with CapturaTalk

SPEECH RECOGNITION AND text-to-speech software can help pupils with dyslexia to access text. The trouble is they keep learners tied to their laptops. What about if they are out and about? A mobile phone with CapturaTalk could be the answer.

CapturaTalk turns a mobile phone into a text reader. Point it at some text, take a picture and hear the words. Pupils can use it to access all sorts of information: a notice at an exhibition, a safety poster on work experience or a handout. CapturaTalk scans and identifies the text and reads out the information. It will also save the scanned file for future use.

Harry is in Year 10 at Richard Lander School in Truro. He was identified as having dyslexia when he was still in primary school. He has received different types of support all through secondary school including withdrawal for small group support work. However, when he was moving to KS4 a new strategy was needed. Steve Harris is the Learning Support Team Leader at the school. He explained: 'It worked well for Harry to be taken out of some classes at KS3 but now with GCSEs looming, he could not afford to

miss any time in the classroom so we cast around for another strategy.'

At the same time, the county dyslexia co-ordinator was introducing CapturaTalk and

You could ...

✔ Provide information cards for pupils to identify clues for a treasure trail

✔ Send emails for pupils to obtain information to help with their homework (they can use the software to read emails and documents sent to the phone)

✔ Provide opportunities to read labels on products to discover the ingredients or purpose of the products

✔ Put a series of objects in boxes with descriptions on the outside to see if pupils can identify what is in the box

✔ Label objects in a display to allow pupils to discover which object is which

looking for schools which might be interested in trying the phone and software to see if they worked well with secondary-aged pupils. Harry seemed to be the ideal candidate and when it was suggested to him, he jumped at the chance. 'Part of the reason why we chose him was that he was already using voice recognition software and so was quite confident about using technology,' said Steve. 'He is also an intelligent boy, although he really struggles with his reading. He was recently tested again by the education psychologist and there is a very clear discrepancy between his IQ and his reading age.'

With CapturaTalk, Harry takes a picture of the text and has it read back to him through his headphones. He decided early on that he would not use it in all lessons: he uses it for Science, and Design and Technology where he is working on Food Science. The reason why he has chosen these areas is that they tend to have text which is in numbered points or in short paragraphs.

This is important because Harry found early on that it is not easy to capture large chunks of text on an image and transfer them to the screen. In other lessons where there is more dense text, he found that it was too disruptive and time-consuming for him to take a series of pictures, transfer them, listen to them and then take more pictures, so his strategy in those lessons is to ask for someone to read the text to him in a continuous stream.

'We like CapturaTalk,' said Steve, 'because we want to ensure that our learners are as independent as possible and we focus a lot on finding strategies that work for individuals.'

Key points

1. For the best quality sound, use the best headphones possible.
2. It works best with short chunks of text, not solid blocks.
3. It is less reliable in poor light.

Contacts and information

http://www.capturatalk.com/
http://iansyst.com/

Brilliant Idea 7

Put comics in the mix: improving narrative skills

COMIC BOOKS HAVE been blamed for declining standards in reading and writing and are sometimes viewed as not being proper books, but one school in Coventry has used them as part of their focus on improving the quality of writing, particularly among boys, ultimately lifting a critical number of pupils from level 3 into level 4.

Grangehurst is a large primary school in the north east of Coventry. The proportion of pupils eligible for free school meals is above average, as is the number identified as having learning difficulties or disabilities. About a fifth of pupils come from minority ethnic backgrounds although only a small number are in the early stages of learning English.

The school involved in this project had identified the raising of boys' attainment and the need to adopt more varied and interactive teaching styles as one of their main priorities. The project was based in two parallel Year 5 classes who were working on Narrative Unit 2: Traditional Stories, Fables, Myths and Legends. The classes were of mixed ability, but contained a number of children who were underachievers. The teachers identified a group of underachieving children to target and track through the project. The majority of children in this group were boys.

The unit allowed for lots of cross-curricular ideas involving design and technology, history and science linked around the Robin Hood theme. At the writing phase children were offered a choice of ways to produce their own stories – *The Adventures of Robin Hood* – and all stories were to be published in a class book.

The use of ICT to produce a comic strip of their stories was highly motivating and the children were immensely proud of their work. This work also helped them to develop a good sense of a plot. One teacher reported: 'The children loved doing the comics. The fact that the pictures were of themselves made them even more interested and they were so proud of their work when they saw them printed. The comics helped children to get familiar with the story they were going to write and to separate narrative from speech. They were able to think about what was important to put into the speech bubbles, which then helped them later in

their writing to think out about the dialogue they would use.'

Whitmore Junior School in Basildon has used Comic Life for Social and Emotional aspects of Learning (SEAL). Pupils took the theme of rumours and produced a podcast and comic book to show how rumours and gossip could hurt people's feelings. They gathered together visuals and produced a script. One of the pupils said, 'All you do is drag pictures into a box click onto a button and speech bubbles come up. Then you type in text and it turns into comic book.'

Teacher Peter Everett said, 'This gives them the opportunity to try something completely different and they don't realise how much their learning has developed as a result.'

You could ...

✔ Use comic strips to relate any kind of narrative: eyewitness accounts for humanities or retelling a fairy tale, for example

✔ Use for sequencing work for science or cookery with key ideas in speech bubbles

✔ Create stories about Greek myths and legends (www.e2bn.org have a wonderful story creator)

✔ Create warning posters with captions

✔ Create your own comic strip guide book to your school

✔ Create labels for use around the school to turn off lights or taps

✔ Create your own comic strip for a film or song you like

Contacts and information

Comic Life – http://plasq.com
Garfield Comic Creator – http://www.garfield.com/fungames/comiccreator.html
Strip Generator – http://www.stripgenerator.com
Comic Brush – http://www.comicbrush.com
Comic Life and SEAL – http://www.heppell.net/bva/bva4/whitmorejunior.htm
How to use Comic Life in the Classroom – http://www.macinstruct.com/node/69
Children at Hackleton School using Comic Life at Silverstone –
    http://www.youtube.com/watch?v=JEQVYr-7MbU

Brilliant Idea 8

Dance your way to fitness

PHYSICAL ACTIVITY IS a very important ingredient for good health. However some pupils have poor body image and lack confidence in their ability to play games or take part in gym activities. Many children are natural couch potatoes while others have physical disabilities or degenerative conditions which make it hard to maintain levels of fitness. There is a solution: Let's Dance!

Tamworth School Sport Partnership has introduced the Fitness Gaming Just for Schools dance mats to engage those pupils who do not enjoy PE. Feedback from pupils has often been that they don't like sport or that they do not like being directed by a teacher. In Tamworth they hope that by providing an activity which is more in line with out-of-school interests, they will increase the popularity of physical activity. The company also provides practice mats; this gets round the problem of what other pupils do while one child is performing. Audiences can get restive and it is a good idea to nip potential discipline problems in the bud so the practice mats are a welcome chance for preparation and rehearsal.

Streetly Sports College in Walsall is using the Cyber Coach system to solve several problems: to re-engage girls who are turned off by competitive team games; provide individualised lessons and offer a structured programme of activities. Staff like the system as it provides an effective way of ensuring that when teachers are absent they can offer cover classes that work well. Cyber Coach has also proved successful with parents who want some exercise after dropping their children at school: Denbighshire County Council has used Cyber Coach systems to push forward their Parents Involved With Schools scheme.

Rob Laird, Partnership Development Manager at Streetly Sports College, is also optimistic that Cyber Coach will motivate a difficult group : 'We have a very low ability disaffected group of boys who are being held back because they do not possess the physical fitness and social skills of their peers. It was essential that we found something that would alleviate the problems they were experiencing, help them feel less pressurised to achieve, and enable them to work at their own level. We were looking for something they could enjoy succeeding in and improve on their grades. They needed a new initiative to re-engage them with PE lessons'.

The Cyber Coach system includes a 'Virtual Dance Instructor' which features many different dance routines. The Virtual Dance Instructor has been used a lot with pupils choosing sessions such as Combat, Marine, Salsa, Hip Hop, Bollywood, Aerobics, Step, Street, Tai Chi and Disco. Some sessions have covered some interesting combinations of the above!

But what about pupils with muscular dystrophy or cerebral palsy, or those in a wheelchair? The Partnership has just purchased two special mats so that some pupils with disabilities can be fully integrated into these lessons. Barbara O' Sullivan, Paediatrician Physiotherapist for Walsall, is a fan: 'The children liked the hand-held dance mats. The children who weren't ambulant were able to use Cyber Coach in their wheelchairs. Every child there said it was great. The girls loved the dance aspect and it was something they could use. They could still interact with the other kids whilst in the wheelchair and participate in computer style games.'

They say dance mats ...

1. Engage those pupils who do not currently enjoy PE
2. Let pupils set their own challenges
3. Are very visual and so work well for pupils who find it hard to follow spoken instructions
4. Are seen as a fun activity and not as physical exercise
5. Can help pupils who are losing mobility in their lower bodies to remain active

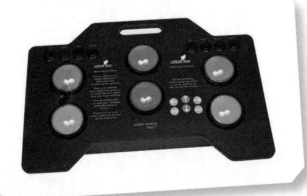

You could ...

✔ Host inter-school competitions

✔ Use in after-school clubs

✔ Use dance mats with a Wii

✔ Make it a feature of transition activities where primary and secondary pupils come together

✔ Hold community events

✔ Host a dance-a-thon

✔ Use for Tai Chi

✔ Get pupils to develop a cheerleading routine

✔ Use for pupils with weight issues as part of a fitness regime

Contacts and information

http://www.fitnessgaming.co.uk/
http://www.cyber-coach.co.uk/

Brilliant Idea 9

Digital video for life stories

IT SEEMS TO be that digital storytelling as a medium is well suited to fostering a sense of kinship and community. It has an immediate appeal because it combines images, sound and text and gives us the sense of drawing back the curtain on someone else's life if only for a few moments.

Brendan Routledge, a consultant with Suffolk Education Consultants, has worked with schools across the East of England and believes digital storytelling can change lives. Here he describes two instances where the end result more than justified the time and effort teachers and pupils put into learning how the technology worked.

Sinead was in Year 6 at Bishop Parker Primary School in Milton Keynes. She was unhappy, had a very poor self-image and was sidelined by many of her classmates. She never completed any work and was struggling both academically and socially. The school took part in a pilot project on digital storytelling run by the East of England Broadband Network. The brief was to tell a story, which had to be true, and produce pictures or ideas for video clips which could be shot very quickly.

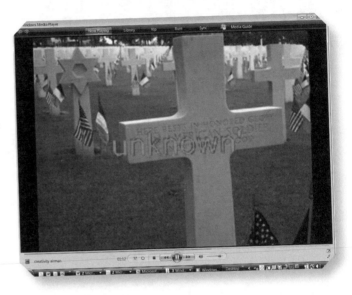

For some reason, this really captured Sinead's imagination and she told the story of her dog Rex from his days as a puppy, chewing her teddies and Barbies, through to his death. A lovable rogue, he brought down the curtains and opened the bathroom window until he got too old. When her story was shown to the rest of the class they saw her in a different light. She had become an individual and not just the surly girl at the back of the class who did as little as possible. Some of the boys started asking her to help them construct their Storyboards and to decide what to include and how to tell their stories. Her confidence grew and this changed her attitude to reading and writing. She started to do things of her own accord instead of hanging back and feeling a failure.

Digital storytelling can also bridge the gap between generations. During the Second World War, there was an American airbase at Mendlesham. Stoke Ash primary School in Suffolk used this for a KS2 project. They looked at local history books, correspondence and archive records. The pupils also visited the American War Cemetery at Madingley, near Cambridge, where they found the graves of airmen who had been based at their airfield. Last year they met a number of the veterans on their annual visit to the airfields of East Anglia. The pupils produced digital stories based on individual airmen, particular planes and a tour of the airfield then and now. They also linked poems written by one of the airmen with digital

Contacts and information

Windows Movie Maker is free on most Windows machines.
However, schools may prefer to use iMovie (Mac), Pinnacle Studio, Premiere Elements or Revelation Sight & Sound from Logotron.
They are all based on the same storyboard or timeline technology which is essential for planning and use the same special effects and transitions so pupils find it easy to transfer their skills.
Suffolk Education Consultants – http://www.suffolkeducationconsultants.net/

images. The stories were eventually turned into a DVD with additional material, including video clips from a memorial service held at the school which was attended by senior US Air Force officers.

'The head teacher was able to travel to USA in September and present the finished work to the veterans at their annual reunion,' said Brendan. 'This was a very emotional experience. The veterans were overwhelmed by the interest taken in their stories and by the quality of the work produced by such young children. Certainly this technology offers a rich resource and way of working for pupils who are not succeeding with more conventional methods.'

What makes a good digital story?

1. It should be short – people get restless after a few minutes and the story loses its power.
2. The best examples are based on personal experiences so that we learn something about the individual storytellers, their life and their attitudes.
3. Go for a few carefully chosen images, a voice-over and/or background music and simple titling. Don't let the technology overwhelm the story.
4. Find sources of copyright-free music. In Suffolk the Regional Broadband Consortia (RBC) has entered into an agreement with the music production company Audio Network plc.
5. Get good pictures: these might be digital camera, scanned or drawn but the more pictures you have to choose from the better the end result.
6. Don't let the work drag on. Many pupils can make something quite good in a short space of time. Too much time leads to loss of impetus.

You could ...

✔ Make videos about your daily routine, family, school or people who help us

✔ Use a green screen behind your video to enable pupils to present information or stories while putting a photo behind them. Kudlian's I Can Present makes this very easy

✔ Make a story starter video and ask 'what happens next?'

✔ Make video clips of a story and then ask students to put them in order

✔ Ask pupils to make the letters in their names with their bodies and use as a quiz for the rest of the class

✔ Take videos through different shape 'masks'...a keyhole, a door, a spyglass

Brilliant Idea 10

Tell me all about it: recording pupils' voices in place of writing!

S OME CHILDREN FIND the task of recording their work through writing just too difficult. Teachers need to show what the child knows – up until now, writing it down has been the only option. But how about recording their observations or knowledge using a basic microphone/recorder such as the Easi-Speak?

Recording children's voices used to be hard work. Often a learning support assistant would sit in the corner of the room and press buttons while holding a microphone and urging a child to speak. The quality was not always good and it was very much a discrete activity cut off from the main classroom. Now it is so easy to integrate sound into a lesson in a much more natural way and 'roving' microphones let you record on the move and then plug into the computer once you are back in the classroom.

Crays Hill School in Essex has a high traveller intake. The KS1 teacher took the pupils out on a bug hunt using Easi-Speak microphones. At the end of the day the children sat enthralled as they listened to their classmates' descriptions and tried to identify their bug on a chart in the classroom.

'All at once,' their teacher said, 'children who would switch off in normal lessons were listening attentively, absorbing and retaining information and priding themselves on being first to identify the bug! So much follow-up work ensued, from charts and graphs to recorded stories about bugs. It was so much fun to see all the class included in the activities!'

Advantages

These digital voice recorders are very robust so you can use them with children of all ages as they will stand a few knocks. There is a built-in microphone and speaker and you can record, play back and skip files. Recordings can be made directly to MP3 which makes podcasting very easy or to WAV format and can be downloaded to a computer via USB.

You could ...

- ✔ Use it to record, upload and re-record projects to assess progress
- ✔ Use it for recording interviews, plays and information such as cooking activities
- ✔ Record in your times table songs and rhymes for all the class to sing to
- ✔ Use it to present mock radio programmes or school news items
- ✔ Interview local residents or visitors to the school
- ✔ Use it on field trips to record observations and reactions to different environments
- ✔ Record and listen to music and sounds
- ✔ Get the children's first reactions about sports days, singing or being in a school production

Contacts and information
www.tts-group.co.uk/

18

Brilliant Idea 11

Seeing is believing

HEAD INTO THE supermarket, walk past the vegetables and then saunter towards the deli counter. What about some snacks or biscuits or maybe fresh orange juice? The Bridge at Hadley Learning Community in Telford has benefited from an incredible piece of immersive technology. Amazing Interactives uses a 'REACH OUT' 3D system. Their latest Life Skills Supermarket module bears an uncanny resemblance to Sainsbury's and lets pupils walk around, see products and feel as if they are really there.

The Bridge is a special school with 162 pupils aged 5 to 19 years. It provides for pupils with severe and profound learning disabilities. Many of them have additional needs including physical difficulties, sensory impairment and autism. In addition, there is an assessment nursery for up to 40 part-time pupils. The school is also a Business and Enterprise College giving pupils a chance to find out about tourism, creative industries, fair trade and to run mini enterprises.
http://www.hadleylearningcommunity.org.uk
www.telford.gov.uk

The Amazing Interactives software has proved very successful and led them in new directions. Originally they used it for life skills and way finding. Pupils had to navigate and find their way round, deciding which aisle to go down. They also had to identify products, so for example, they were presented with a shopping list and had to find the ingredients needed to make a pizza. They also practised their functional skills, e.g. maths, considering prices, working with money, till receipts and special offers, such as two for one, or buy two get one free.

For some pupils it provided practice in going shopping. They could have a go before trying the real thing. However, some pupils do not cope with the bustle and noise of a real supermarket so the Amazing Interactives experience could help them get used to the environment or could provide an alternative experience.

Diane Hasell is assistant head of the Bridge School and reported that there were several unexpected advantages: 'We received 3D cameras as part of the project and have been using them to film the students in a whole range of activities. We have also shared the technology with two local primary schools and a local private special school. In return, we get to use their grounds for some of our other projects.

'Although the Supermarket is an expensive technology, it is well worth the investment. It is neither entertainment nor edutainment, but it certainly does entertain and engage our learners.'

You could ...

✔ Go online and find out how to get shopping delivered

✔ Look at shopping apps for iPads and smart phones

✔ Create a commentary to go with the virtual supermarket tour

Contacts and information
http://www.amazinginteractives.com/

Mathletics: bringing a competitive edge to maths learning

MOTIVATING STUDENTS IN maths lessons can be a real challenge. It is also difficult to find programs which cover a range of topics at different levels. At the Cotswold Community School in Wiltshire, they have found that Mathletics has raised the profile of maths and produced individualised lessons.

Mathletics is an online resource used by pupils all across the world. It contains hundreds of activities for pupils aged 5–18. There are mental arithmetic challenges and materials linked to concepts and topics from the full KS1–5 national curriculum, ranging from counting and comparing in Year 1 to perimeter area and volume in Year 5 to linear modelling in Year 12.

Cotswold Community School is an independent ESBD school catering for boys from Year 4 to Year 11.

Elizabeth Moore, Mathematics Co-ordinator said: 'This program has totally changed maths lessons for both our unmotivated and motivated students. We teach boys who have a wide variety of ability and behaviour. The lessons which we set to each boy's own level have made our work so much richer. They can either "learn online" if a teacher is absent or, after a topic is learnt, they can test their own knowledge. Mathletics can even be accessed at home and could provide homework and further evidence.'

There is support at the touch of a button and one of the best features is that all lessons can be printed out. The hard copy shows all the questions – marked for you – and the corrections are shown for the students. This tool provides all teachers with evidence that is named and dated. We can see pupil progress very easily.

Then there is Live Mathletics, where they compete in mental maths questions with students from other countries (shown on a spinning map of the world). From the anticipation of which country they are competing with, to the participation of the 'race' and finally the result – if they have won, it is fantastic; if they have not, they can immediately try again.

All the boys have gained so much confidence from using their own set lessons and Live Mathletics and now they often choose to learn 'on Mathletics please'.

FAQs

Do you need to pay for Mathletics to join in World Maths Day or is there a promotion to encourage schools to join?
World Maths Day is a completely free event. Teachers are encouraged to enter their classes and individual students can also enter. Even teachers can participate! Visit www. worldmathsday.com to register yourself or your school. Schools who are already subscribed to Mathletics can sign in with their existing usernames and passwords.

How can I go online and compete with other countries?
Students sign into www.worldmathsday.com to play. They will be automatically matched up with students of a similar age and ability from anywhere in the world!

How do you link up with them?
World Maths Day is an online platform. Students will be automatically matched with up to three other children when they select to play a game.

Can you print out class certificates or individual certificates for pupils?
Yes, every student who takes part will be able to print out a special participation certificate. There will also be special prizes for the top performing schools, classes and students.

Contacts and information

http://www.mathletics.co.uk/
Grays School in Thurrock and the Maths Challenge –
    http://www.youtube.com/watch?v=uofLx9dCkIo

Brilliant Idea 13

Chatting about Miss Havisham

IT IS SOMETIMES hard to motivate students, so tapping into interests such as online chat can be a really good way to engage them. Anna Hughes taught poetry to a mixed ability Year 8/9 transition group who were about to start their GCSE course at Caludon Castle School in Coventry. Here she reports on how using a wiki had unexpected results.

'The first step of the project was to create and develop the webspace. Although this sounds daunting, it really isn't difficult. I was pleasantly surprised at how quickly I got to grips with it.' (See the 'How to use a Wiki' help sheet if you are interested in setting up your own.)

'The transition scheme that I was using with my year 8s had a section on poetry with a focus on the poem "Havisham" by Carol Ann Duffy. I uploaded the poem to the wiki and created a page with a number of resources that I would normally have delivered to the class myself: a PowerPoint about the poem which I had previously delivered to other classes, a set of questions, some notes in a Word document and two links to useful websites which analysed the poem. I showed the students how to use the site, got them signed up with their own usernames and then they had to use the resources to answer some fairly difficult questions.

'I also briefly introduced the students to the discussion pages and encouraged them to communicate with each other. This worked amazingly well because it gave them an opportunity to share their views or ask questions that they wouldn't necessarily have wanted to do in the open classroom. It helped that they could hide behind their "online identity". I knew who they were as I had access to everyone's username, but other students didn't (unless they decided to share this with others) so they took a risk and had a go at parts of the poem that they found hard.

'Some pupils were contributing when normally they would have kept quiet. If I had taught them the poem, they would have followed my guidance and most likely would have ended up with my interpretation of the poem. Instead, they came up with really unusual, original responses. Most importantly, students were now

interrogating the poem themselves, asking questions and explaining things to each other. A number of students posted questions asking for help reading the meaning of different lines from the poem; these were promptly answered and explained by others in the class. Suddenly, it seemed there was no need for me!'

This case study is based on a project undertaken for the National Association for Teaching English (NATE).

A fuller version can be accessed at: www.nate.org.uk/htt. We are grateful to NATE for their permission to include the project here.

Contacts and information
http://primarypad.com/

You could ...

✔ Make an online collaborative space to examine a problem such as bullying, making friends or other SEAL topics

✔ Use a debating forum for a current topic in the news

✔ Use to provide the background for a topic being studied in school i.e. ask students to find out as much as they can about China and then review the results the next day

Brilliant Idea 14

iMovie supports the curriculum

SOME CHILDREN HAVE very highly developed visual skills. These days they may be exposed to television very early and learn more through this medium than via books, radio or even conversation. Some experts claim that YouTube is beginning to challenge Google as a search engine as young people look for information in a visual form.

At Orwell High School in Felixstowe, Food Technology teacher Nick Day was tearing his hair out over his Year 8 group. 'They were really good at the practical work,' he said, 'but they could not write it up.' Often they would just get as far as writing the date and title before inspiration failed. He was interested in used digital video to record progress and showed them how everything worked.

After a quick demonstration, pupils were left to make apple crumble and then they used digital cameras to chronicle each stage of the process before recording a voice-over. The end result is excellent. It includes demonstrations, descriptions of processes as well as an evaluation and it can be used as a resource for future classes. This was their first attempt at working in this way but despite not being familiar with the technology, it took them no longer to make their digital record than it took the rest of the class to write up results on paper. 'This is an important point,' said Nick, 'because if it takes two hours to do then it will be a non-starter in most classrooms but this is an immediate and very direct method of capturing and recording achievements.'

At Frank Wise School in Banbury, iMovie and digital video have become a mainstay of the school's approach to the curriculum, says Head Teacher Sean O'Sullivan. 'We can use it for practice activities which we will not store so children who struggle with speech can have several goes and we can cut the best bits and build a sentence. They can do a voice over anything which gives variety and motivates them to keep trying,' said Sean. 'Using slow motion has been a great way to draw attention to a key point. For example, we might roll a toy car down a slope and then do it again on a rougher surface to show the impact of friction but if a child is looking away the point is lost. We can play it back in slow motion so they really focus on what is on screen.'

He is amazed by the digital literacy of his pupils: 'Although our pupils have learning disabilities, that does not necessarily mean they are slow learners. Sometimes they get stuff really quickly. One boy was editing a clip of himself swimming. It was shorter than the music track he had chosen so he just used copy and paste to make it longer. I was just amazed. It was so intuitive for him.'

You could ...

✔ Make a one-minute video for each hour of the school day

✔ Create a live morning news show

✔ Record science experiments

✔ Create a digital record of your local community

✔ Transfer clips between home and school to help prompt answers to, 'What did you do ...?'

Contacts and information
www.frankwise.oxon.sch.uk/
www.apple.com

Brilliant Idea 15

Keeping pupils 'in the zone'

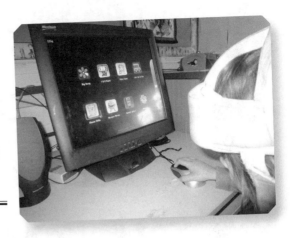

HOW DO YOU give children access to programs and activities without letting them loose on the computer? At Fairfield School, Batley, they are using MyZone to ensure children make purposeful choices.

Chloe is 7 and has a lot of health issues. She has seizures and some days she is a very poorly child. On those days she just likes to have a go with Choose and Tell Nursery Rhymes which let her make choices but are not too taxing. On her brighter days, she uses a mouse and enjoys clicking around the screen. MyZone makes sure that she only accesses what her teachers want her to access. Left to her own devices, she would be searching for CBeebies online but with MyZone, she stays focused on her work and gets lots done.

Chloe attends Fairfield School, a community school in Batley which caters for children aged 3–19 with severe learning difficulties and profound and multiple learning difficulties. Most of them are switch users and many have communication difficulties too. The school was finding that some children managed to wander away from whatever task had been set and got lost in cyberspace. They started off with a free program which stopped children from accessing the web or altering the teacher settings but then they discovered MyZone from Inclusive Technology, which came with lots of useful programs and activities ideal for their learners.

MyZone sits on the desktop and is very visual with photographs of the pupil, pictures and large buttons. It can be operated with a mouse, tracker ball, touch screen or switches. As part of the bundle there are 12 simple games, including Sandcastle Builder; Making Music, Colouring In and Mosaic, but others can easily be added.

Rosie Murphy, Communication Manager at Fairfield School, said it has worked well for their pupils. The school has set it up with SwitchIT programs, Big Bang, Target and Touch, cause and effect activities that provide much needed practice for switch users. They have now added 2Paint from 2Simple software which enables children with limited motor skills to create wonderful colourful compositions.

Teachers can set up MyZone for individual pupils so they have a suite of programs, activities, games, and web pages suited to their needs or to the topic they are working on. For example, they might have sets of photographs and web pages for a science topic or a day out. Some children will just have one icon on the desktop, others might have as many as 12. They can navigate between pages using the on screen arrows but when they close a program or website they return to MyZone. Now they can't wander off or get lost!

You could ...

✔ Try the MyZone games on a touch monitor or interactive whiteboard, including Big Bus; Colouring In; Keyboard; Tops, Middles and Bottoms; Mosaic; Making Music; Sandcastle Builder; Pizza Maker; Train Tracker

Contacts and information

http://www.inclusivetlc.com/

See a demo of the Touch Monitor and MyZone – http://www.youtube.com/watch?v=DUWndRmN7kU or go to a search engine and type: Inclusive MyZone YouTube

Radio freedom: make a podcast and take control of the airwaves!

MANY PUPILS HAVE difficulties with speaking and listening. Some pupils are not very articulate and struggle to express their views so they go for simple blunt statements which do not reflect the complexity of their thinking. There are different ways of drawing them out without making them feel they are being singled out for attention.

At Frank Wise School in Banbury, the leavers' class, known as the *10th Family Group* enjoy podcasting every Wednesday morning. One topic they featured was a new scanner at the local hospital. This had been covered by their local paper *The Banbury Guardian* and everyone in the group had recorded a response to the article. Sean O'Sullivan, head teacher at the school, recommends using enhanced podcasting. This lets him put in pupil photos to go with each recording. This is really helpful as it focuses attention and reminds everyone whose contribution they are listening to.

It has also proved to be an excellent choice for mixed ability classes in primary schools. Rebecca Cole a teacher at Glenaire Primary School in Shipley answers questions about podcasting:

What do you use?

Podium (Lightbox Education). We dabbled with Audacity which is free but Podium does all the sparkly things we need it to do in a much simpler format. We needed something effective AND intuitive and sometimes you have to pay for that!

What topics have you covered?

Examples for KS1 included poems and stories from the literacy work and Mother's Day Messages – children recorded a personal message and put the link in their cards (you can hear them now on www.glenaire.bradford.sch.uk).

KS2 recorded a whole class debate on circuses linked to persuasive writing in literacy and a dual language story for our partner school near Paris to listen to. They also interviewed a gentleman who had been an evacuee in the Second World War. The children prepared questions they'd like to ask him and we recorded it. He was over the moon and the children were so engaged and keen to be professional.

We also run a Podcasting Club at lunchtime where children can propose, record, edit and publish news stories. These include topical news, a newsround summary of serious and amusing stories as well as the latest pop/fashion/TV/sport news that appeals to them.

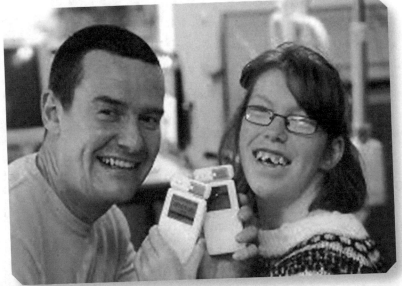

You could make ...

✔ A recorded guide for the school

✔ Interviews

✔ Stories or collaborative stories (pass the mic around from child to child to carry on the story)

✔ Instructions

✔ An account of a day trip

✔ Advertisements and jingles

✔ Mother's Day messages or any special messages

✔ A day in... (a different country/place/era in history/planet)

✔ A Newsround summary

What are the advantages of podcasting?

1. We try to give children a reason to write, speak and listen by giving them an audience.
2. It's fun – children don't think they're working!
3. Encouraging speaking at a young age encourages confidence.
4. It's interactive and therefore engaging.
5. It embraces new technology – there's no point in trying to fight the technology children use – we need to get on board with them and use it too. They love it – so should we!
6. Parents can enjoy hearing what children are doing without having to wait for parents' evenings and open days.

Contacts and information

www.frankwise.oxon.sch.uk/
www.glenaire.bradford.sch.uk
Podium – http://www.podiumpodcasting.com/
Radiowaves – http://www.radiowaves.co.uk/

Brilliant Idea 17

The 'I' in iPod: personalised learning

IPODS ARE ONE of the most popular multimedia devices. Some schools are finding that iPods can be used for anytime, anyplace learning that supports a variety of learning styles. Pupils need very few ICT skills and can access video and sound files or use them as a recording device.

The iPod can inspire and engage students of all abilities. Audio files can be broken down and used as aural sequencing tasks – these are very good for learners with dyslexia. The teacher can also make JPEG image files to cover the content in an exam paper so pupils start to think in exam mode.

Sarah Clark, deputy head, and Lynn O'Brien, ICT co-ordinator, have used iPods with pupils at Isobel Mair School in East Renfrewshire, Scotland. iPods play an important role within the curriculum. Students frequently use the iPod Shuffle for a range of things, including listening to music; this acts as a huge motivator. Audio books are recorded onto iPods and pupils who do not have the ability to read can listen to a story via spoken word and receive a copy on digital format.

'Last year we focused on *The Lion, The Witch and The Wardrobe* and recorded chapters of the book onto the iPod. These were then taken home to listen to; due to the trendy and modern association with iPods it meant students were not embarrassed, which removed the potential stigma that could be attached,' said Sarah Clark. 'We use iPod classics to support both learners and staff. Students are able to create videos of themselves travelling independently for example, which is thoroughly motivating because they enjoy watching the videos. Not only does this reinforce teaching and learning, it also improves parental engagement as they can share with parents what they have been doing at school.'

Students are also provided with an iPod Touch to support teaching and learning, and of course, to have some fun. As the iPod is portable, they are able to use it in a flexible manner at home and in school. For non-verbal students they are currently trialling an application based communication system called Proloquo2Go. Using the app on the iPod Touch which

has a built in speaker, this enables the iPod to be used as a portable communication system.

Adam Parker, a teacher at Aylesford School and Language College in Warwickshire, used iPods to improve science learning. The aim was to engage disaffected boys in revision activities using non-traditional methods. Many students had iPods, but only used them for music. He felt that iPods could, 'get revision materials into the pockets' of his pupils. He divided a Year 9 group with a broad ability range into mixed non-friendship groups of no more than four. He let them choose one of the following curriculum areas to work on:

1.   Cell structure and function, and specialised cells
2.   States of matter and changing states
3.   Forces, including balanced and unbalanced forces.

Students had a one-hour lesson to plan how they would deliver the content of the curriculum area using either PowerPoint presentations, audio notes, multiple choice quizzes. After that, they had two one-hour lessons to create their resource and review their project. The files created were uploaded to the school's learning platform and were made available to all students within Year 9.

You could ...

✔ Put video and audio lessons onto the iPods for the students and parents to be able to access at home

✔ Use the iPod as a video portfolio. They were able to shoot video of themselves and the students performing a specific skill and then send it home to the parents

✔ Record a simple voice memo and send it home to parents

✔ Use it to help pupils and parents practise Makaton or British Sign Language (BSL) signs at home

Contacts and information

http://www.ea.e-renfrew.sch.uk/isobelmair/
http://www.aylesford-elearning.net/core/index.php

Brilliant Idea 18

Yes, Wii can: turn-taking and getting fit

SCHOOLS ARE TRYING to find ways to combat the growing problem of obesity. Some children have medical conditions which mean they put on weight very easily and it can be hard to find physical activities for children with poor coordination or physical disabilities. The Nintendo Wii is one solution, as Dorin Park School in Cheshire found.

Many people think of the Wii as a hobby to be pursued at home. Others see it as a device targeted at able bodied people so it might surprise you to know that during the last two years a successful 'Wii-therapy' has been launched in the Peto Institute for children whose motor impairments originate from damage to the central nervous system.

Dorin Park is a specialist SEN college for pupils aged 2-19. They were lucky enough to receive a Wii from MGL, an education and technology support company. Sarah Patchitt is the ICT co-coordinator at the school and was delighted at the prospect of using it to encourage pupils to have a go at bowling. She quickly discovered that it could develop a whole host of skills: physical, social and cognitive.

First of all there are motor skills. Holding a controller pushing the buttons improves pupils' coordination and fine motor skills while smashing a tennis ball or bowling a ball towards skittles requires full arm movement which helps with gross motor skills. The activities also help with social skills as pupils learn choice making and turn-taking.

Some of them got very creative making a Wii Mii ('wee me'), an avatar or digitised emblem of a player which represents them in the on-screen world. 'We spent lessons developing their own little characters,' said Sarah. 'It developed their self-image and made them feel very positive. It was fun and raised self-esteem.' The games can also provide opportunities for numeracy as they can count the skittles falling down or work out their score. Pupils find it very motivating and if they are motivated they try harder. In fact Dorin Park is using the Wii to assess pupils for their P levels.

Using the Wii lets students enjoy new experiences: 'They can hold a tennis racquet and hit a ball,' says Sarah. 'In real life they can't.' Not only can pupils enjoy doing these things, she adds, they can enjoy doing them well. 'The pupils are for once competing on a level playing field. I've got a Wii at home but I still can't beat them.'

You could ...

✔ Record pupils' pulse rates before and after exertion

✔ Create a symbol sheet for them to record their feelings

✔ Use Excel to create charts to interpret that data

✔ Film some of the pupils using the wii, script and record a voice over

✔ Scripting and record either an audio or video interview

✔ Schedule a breakfast Wii Fit class at 8:15 in the morning to improve punctuality

They say the Wii ...

1. Improves ability to cope with new tasks and learning new skills
2. Improves non verbal reasoning skills
3. Helps with cardio vascular fitness
4. Keeps children more mentally and physically active
5. Introduces challenges and risk taking in controlled environment helps control obesity
6. Improves motor skills balance and coordination

With thanks to Dan McKeown.

Contacts and information
http://www.mymgl.com/

Brilliant Idea 19

Band identity: music and marketing

WITH PROGRAMMES SUCH as *The Apprentice*, children are familiar with the concept of creating a product and marketing it. It brings together research, planning, writing, collaborating, presenting and evaluation. Even better there is a host of models for children to draw on so they can move into role play or acting out a part and feel less exposed.

Band in a Box is a 13 week project for Year 6 pupils at Gavinburn School in Dumbarton. It is an exciting and even glamorous project and has been so successful that the school is committed to running it every year for the foreseeable future. Head teacher Gillian Penney says: 'This immensely popular project has helped pupils to develop their skills. Often those who find conventional literacy activities just reinforce their sense of inadequacy seem to flourish in this activity.'

Year 6 is divided into small mixed ability teams which have a series of tasks to complete. First, they form a band and allocate roles. They might be themselves or create an alter ego. Using GarageBand they have to compose a song. They then have to create

their marketing materials. Storyboards require pupils to plan and compose, to put forward and justify their creative ideas.

Naturally it's soon time for the band to go on tour so before heading to Europe they have to use the internet to find flights and a suitable hotel. Next they use I Can Present, to show off their skills. It is an application designed to bring students presentations to life by allowing them to create film and present their work in a new and exciting way using green screen technology. They can film their band or they might choose to create a digital animation.

The children are already familiar with green screen technology as they have used it for other projects such as reporting on an alien landing for *Dr Who* or a live broadcast of a historical event. The more confident will talk direct to camera perhaps having memorised a script or by improvising. Others will use the autocue function to stop them from drying up.

Of course as a highly successful band they won't be home in time for the MTV awards so they need to record their acceptance speech. 'It's amazing how many American accents creep in at this stage,' laughs head teacher Gillian Penny. Finally there are the real awards as the school hosts a black tie red carpet event with awards for all from best production to best song.

'Last year we had a boy with such serious learning disabilities that we were not sure if he could stay in mainstream but he took part in every task. He was very active in the French broadcast. For once he could work as an equal partner.'

You could ...

✔ Create a product in D&T and run a marketing campaign

✔ Market a twin town

✔ Create a series of vodcasts around the school play or sports day

✔ Think of a fund-raising project and use the ideas to make it a success

Contacts and information

http://www.kudlian.net/products/icanpresent/index.php
www.apple.com/ilife/garageband/

Brilliant Idea 20

Playing by ear: using Textease Studio CT to develop writing skills

**Cheryl Dobbs,
Independent Education
Consultant**

TEXTEASE IS A talking desktop publisher that is designed for whole school use. It can be used with students of all ages and abilities, but it is also ideal for using with students who have difficulty with writing activities or are reluctant to write at all.

Tom is a good talker. He has a lot to say on subjects which interest him. He enjoys using computers and has a number of activities which he enjoys out of school. However, his writing skills are poor. He writes very little but even this is barely legible and is full of spelling errors and crossings out. His writing does not reflect his true intellect.

Textease is a very easy program to learn to use both for students and teachers. It combines the use of a desktop publisher with a talking word processor – both of which provide powerful tools for composition of text and image. The students rapidly learned how to use the many desktop publishing features available within the program such as simple animation features, buttons to link to new pages, adding audio and were eager to produce their own unique texts.

Students were encouraged to make their own talking, interactive books which could be shared with others. These were based upon their own personal interests and were often initiated by images they had collected or created. The images were then used to create the framework of the book to which text or audio was later added. These were then shared with other class members and their own families. This encouraged some parents to purchase a home user

The echidna is a shy animal.

It eats termites and ants. It has a very long sticky tongue.

version so that the same software could be used at home to support other homework activities. The desktop publishing capabilities of Textease enabled students to create exciting documents such as linked pages, simple animation and incorporation of visual imagery easily.

They could hear their words read back to them so that previous errors such as sentence structure or omitted words could be heard when they had been missed by visual scanning alone. Audio recordings could be made directly onto the page. This was used to convey other information when they had become tired or frustrated with their writing and displayed their true cognitive ability and not the limited range that the constructed typed text concealed.

Some students used this recording feature as a type of auditory mindmap, creating prompts for ideas that they would later construct into written text. Since text could be constructed anywhere on the page – this also helped those that had difficulties with planning and structure since they could experiment with its placement.

You could ...

✔ Create personal talking books related to students' specific interests

✔ Use the recording facility to plan work before writing – an auditory planner

✔ Encourage the student to listen to what has been written as part of an editing process

✔ Create mp3 files for pupils to download onto their iPods and use for revision

✔ Use the different voices on the software to present a play or dialogue

Contacts and information
Textease Studio CT – www.textease.co.uk

Brilliant Idea 21

iPads: next generation technology

WHEN SCHOOLS ARE looking to increase their ICT, they often think in terms of interactive whiteboards and laptops or netbooks, but they might want to take a giant step forward and look at using the iPad and free downloadable apps.

At Tennyson Road Primary School in Luton, head teacher Hilary Power has invested in iPads for all the teachers and learning support assistants. In addition there is a set of iPads for small group work and there will soon be some class sets of iPod Touch too. Of course, touch technology is nothing new for children with special needs. Think of switches, touchscreens and interactive whiteboards or Smart Tables.

Hilary has given each teacher an allowance of £25 to spend on apps from the Apple Store. This has been a brilliant strategy because it has encouraged them to explore what's on offer and make decisions about what they need for their class. They like some of the free translation tools. One Polish boy was struggling to find the word he needed so he typed it into the iPad in Polish and they found that he was talking about an animal being 'extinct' – a difficult concept to express without the right vocabulary!

Charlotte Photiades Senco at the school, says Pocket Phonics has been a useful app for children with speech and language problems and for those who are stuck in the early stages of literacy. Pupils can listen to letter sounds and match them to a letter. Then there is Talking Friends where an on-screen cartoon character will repeat back everything you say. This has proven a boon for children learning English as an additional language, children with language delay and some autistic children because it is a fun way of encouraging them to talk.

Kerri McDonald, ICT coordinator, likes the fact that there are apps to use right across the curriculum and for all key stages. There are also lots of talking books. Some feature Disney characters which appeal to children and help them improve listening skills. Simon Says is a good way of improving concentration and memory.

The free Creationary app is great for Design and Technology: roll the dice and select a category from nature, vehicles, buildings or things. Match a picture to a model which is being built of Lego bricks onscreen. It's a way of practising looking at 2D designs and 3D objects.

Contacts and information

Dr Tim Rudd has published a really useful survey of current discussions surrounding the use of the IPad and apps in education – http://www.livelab.org.uk/ and check the resources section.

Lots of useful iPad apps listed here – http://tinyurl.com/6h5gwox

Teachers have responded enthusiastically to the iPad!

1. It switches on and off so easily – no waiting for it to warm up.
2. You can switch it on in odd moments at home and spend just a short time looking at things.
3. It's small and easy to carry around so it goes everywhere.
4. It's robust.
5. It's reliable.
6. It is easy to share ideas with other staff at lunchtime – you don't have to go off and find a machine.
7. Apps are cheap, e.g. 59p.
8. There are lots of free apps.
9. A school could have its own iTunes account so you only pay once for an app but can use it in several classes.
10. The battery lasts 11 hours so you can charge it overnight and it will keep going all day.

You could ...

✔ Download a series of apps and make a 'circuit training' type of activity.

With so many great apps to choose from, select quizzes, games, creative or informative apps to support a topic and allow pupils 10 minutes at each app.

Brilliant Idea 22

Mashing up art

BEV EVANS IS the ICT Coordinator at Pembroke Dock Community School, a large community school in Wales with over 600 pupils. It has an integrated Autistic Centre, which currently has around 24 pupils, mostly boys. Here she talks about ideas for art and animation projects and her new ventures with 2Simple's Purple Mash, a secure creative online space.

We need to have structured sessions and a visual approach to learning can be very important too. Nathan has a fixation with dinosaurs and he has enjoyed creating his own creatures, playing with shapes and textures. He now has a login so that he can carry on creating at home!

Ryan in Year 6 gets very frustrated because he cannot recognise many words or match lower case letters with the upper case letters on a keyboard. Art and animation have opened up ways of telling stories for him he can draw or import pictures and can use a microphone to tell stories. Ryan likes to use 2Create a SuperStory. It is fairly new and it allows pupils to create animated stories and books using simple skills and templates: you can even add your own recorded sound if you're not a confident writer – which is why it is a good choice for a number of pupils within the centre.

Creative ICT can involve looking at different types of computer-based art, graphics and photo editing packages. Pupils can try out many different types of software, some of which are listed below. Even the youngest pupils can enjoy activities like creating repeated animal skin patterns. In an attempt to link their efforts in ICT with a more hands-on activity, you could print out the designs and use wooden animal stencils to cut actual animal shapes out of the appropriate skin patterns.

Pupils use the package 2Paint a Picture in a number of different ways – using the different settings to assist with cross-curricular ideas. For example, the Slice tool can cut and rotate patterns and this has recently been used to help the teaching of symmetry. We have used the Splash tool to create firework pictures. Pupils have also used the Pattern tool to link in with the topic of camouflaged animals very successfully and all the pupils in the centre enjoy using the program at their own pace and are really making good progress. This is partly because the program can be used with a touch screen and the Wet Paint option works just like real paint. Add water to make paint runnier and as one colour runs over another it will change colour just as it would in real life.

Purple Mash from 2Simple is a 'mash up' of tool and projects linked to the National Curriculum all pulled together in an online space. Some of the parts are freely available online while others are only accessible once a school has subscribed. Many of the Purple Mash activities have added elements that make them more inclusive. The writing frames have word banks and prompts to assist pupils with writing and a large number of activities include clip art and photos – great if you've got a pupil who finds drawing with a mouse an issue.

2Publish+ has some great templates, making it simple to produce a brochure or a birthday card etc. and also allows you to cover basic skills like copy, paste and import in a child friendly manner. There are also a number of paint projects and some of the projects include texture pens to add an extra dimension.

In Purple Mash you can mix ICT with D&T which is a marvellous thing! Pupils can create houses and vehicles for a street scene, coloured dice for maths activities and masks for role play. Luke was non-verbal when he came to us from a school in Ireland. He did not see the need to verbalise but in his time with us has moved on from sign language to simple sentences and is now using extended sentences. He loves cars and logged on to AutoTrader to search for cars and knew everything there was to know about make model and year. He had no interest in other sites. He designed a car, chose the colour and shape, printed it out as a net. There's nothing quite like getting the scissors and glue out and making something with your own two hands and the pupils can't wait to print out their efforts and bring them back to the classroom to stick together.

You could ...

✔ Make posters

✔ Make logos

✔ Make a crest

✔ Make collages or words and pictures

✔ Make jigsaws, playing cards, sorting cards

✔ Make modern day cameos, fabric, wallpaper or wrapping paper designs

Contacts and information

Revelation Natural Art – http://www.r-e-m.co.uk/logo/?Titleno=25343
2Paint a Picture – http://www.2simple.com/2paintapicture/
Bomomo – http://bomomo.com/
Brushster – http://www.nga.gov/kids/zone/brushster.htm
SumoPaint – http://www.sumopaint.com/home

Photo editing and manipulation packages

Fotoflexer – http://fotoflexer.com
Tuxpi – http://www.tuxpi.com

Photo collage applications

Andrea Mosaic – http://www.andreaplanet.com/andreamosaic
Shape Collage – http://www.shapecollage.com/
Purple Mash – http://www.purplemash.com/

Pembroke Dock Community School

http://www.pembrokedockschool.org.uk/
Bev Evans writes a blog with lots of classroom ideas –
    http://technostories.wordpress.com/

Brilliant Idea 23

Not just an open book

AMAZON RECENTLY REPORTED that the sale of eBooks has outstripped hardbacks. There is a publishing revolution and the new formats – both eBooks and digital fiction – have advantages for cost-conscious schools and for readers who need a little extra support

Put simply, eBooks are digital or electronic versions of paper books. Instead of being printed onto paper and bound into books, the text is formatted into a digital file and read via a special eBook Reader. Equally, it can be read on a computer screen, an interactive whiteboard or on a handheld device such as a mobile phone. The reader 'turns the pages' by using their keyboard or a mouse. Sometimes the text can be read aloud by screen-reading software and often the size, style and colour of the text can be changed which makes it easier to see. Digital fiction is more like a video game with elements that can be controlled by the user, or reader. The style will be familiar to gamers and may attract some reluctant readers because it suits those who are more comfortable with 'doing', in this case interacting with the story and activating multimedia elements that support the text.

These new forms of fiction have more than novelty value and are popular alternatives to text-based fiction for disaffected pupils and are more accessible than black text on white paper.

Jenny Langley from the Manchester Academy said: 'Initially, we used the I-stars eBooks with lower ability pupils in KS3 as a reward when work was completed. Pupils tend to have an interest in anything that they perceive as unusual so we found this approach really successful in terms of motivation. We then moved on to use them as prompt texts in place of print books for whole class inference and deduction activities and with small reading groups that we withdraw from mainstream classes. The range of eBooks is fantastic for these groups and we have found them more successful than using print books, especially in paired reading sessions. We think this is due, in part, to the familiarity they feel with technology and partly because they see them as more sophisticated and interesting.'

'In group reading sessions, some of the pupils find it difficult to keep up and their concentration flags as a result; reading from a print text presents a prime opportunity for disengagement. The usual on-task rate is around 70 per cent but when using eBooks we have found the on-task rate to be much higher at around 90 per cent. We attribute this to the fact that learners can read at a pace that they are comfortable with and don't lose concentration as easily. This is especially noticeable in low ability groups.'

'For me, the most convincing evidence is that there are more hands up when we ask a question, which I think is due to their increased confidence.'

Some examples of digital fiction are well suited to classroom use. We Tell Stories took six classic titles from the Penguin library, including *Hard Times* by Charles Dickens and *The 39 Steps* and created new versions. Fairy Tales is a quest where the reader selects names for the characters, chooses a travelling companion and influences the outcomes of the story. The 21 Steps is based on Buchan's novel and follows the adventures of Rick as he tries to find out why a

---

Contacts and information

I-stars eBooks – http://istars.education.co.uk/
We Tell Stories – http://wetellstories.co.uk/
Inanimate Alice – http://www.inanimatealice.com

dying stranger knew his name. Readers track his progress via Google Maps as he moves from London to Edinburgh.

Inanimate Alice is a thriller which has a cult following all over the world. It brings together elements of computer gaming – still photography, moving image, drawings, painting, puzzles, music and sound effects with a text-based narrative and is backed up with extensive teaching materials.

Benefits of eBooks and digital fiction

They can be used by more than one teacher or pupil at a time which makes them more cost effective and more environmentally friendly

The text is never dog-eared or shabby.

Pupils can highlight parts of the text, for example parts of speech for word work or metaphors. Pupils can bookmark key points to identify a sequence of events or collect evidence for a character study.

The glossary function in eBooks lets learners look up words or supporting texts with ease which gives pupils more control. With digital fiction pupils can use online tools and search engines.

When working on a text extract, teachers often use photocopied sheets. With eBooks an extract can be

You could ...

✔ Use one of the tales from We Tell Stories on an interactive whiteboard for group reading

✔ Read a book together and start a class blog or wiki (see Brilliant Idea 13)

called up on screen without interrupting the lesson or slowing the pace.

The fact that the font can be altered to suit the reader is also very beneficial especially for learners with dyslexia or sight problems and a huge advantage over printed books.

Pupils can post their own reviews online and see what other people think. In this way, they are exposed to lots of different ideas from people who may have very different experiences and different expectations of stories.

Brilliant Idea 24

Storyboarding for behavioural needs

APPROXIMATELY **10 PER CENT** of children and young people have problems with speech language and communication needs. Sometimes for children with language delay or related conditions, multimedia gets to parts that other programs just don't reach.

The joy of multimedia for many learners is that it does not require good reading skills and as it appeals to a range of learning styles, it can help pupils be more independent. Kar2ouche is a multimedia product which can support creative role play, picture making, storyboarding and animation. Children can record their own voices and start to develop their speaking skills. Listening to increasingly complex texts extends a pupil's vocabulary and helps them to process spoken language. Poor readers can listen and follow text on screen and begin to recognise words while the speech and thought bubbles let pupils write in small bite-size chunks. This can be increased gradually so that pupils produce a paragraph to go in the caption window. Later on they might progress to using the writing frames and scaffolds provided in the education support packs.

There are over 50 different Kar2ouche packs covering many curriculum areas but among the most popular are the Shakespeare titles. Here, pupils can practise a sequencing activity, create character maps and choose music to represent different parts of the play.

Lisa Pittwood, a teacher at Ellesmere College, a Secondary MLD school in Leicester, used Kar2ouche to teach *Romeo and Juliet* and *Macbeth* to KS4 students working towards a Certificate of Achievement in English. 'Our students took to it quickly and were producing parts of the story within minutes. It was quite something to be able to look around the computer suite and see eight students who very rarely are able to work independently, just working away on their own. We had previously worked through the story, using books and videos so the students were able to pick ten main events to produce in a very simple

storyboard form. They then transferred these ideas onto Kar2ouche.

'The most valuable part of the work was the students using their thinking skills to see how they could interpret the parts of the story they had picked. This created discussion about the story and helped enhance their understanding of what they knew and helped them to explore more parts of the story than they would have picked up by just listening or watching a video. The most telling part of their increase in knowledge was shown by a task the students were asked to do after using Kar2ouche, for a piece of coursework. Students who can write fairly independently but usually need help with the structure of their writing produced the most sequenced and structured responses I have ever seen them write and they asked for no help, discussed ideas and helped each other with some words they needed spelling. They were extremely secure in their knowledge of the story and showed an increase in confidence with their writing skills.'

At Heathermount, a specialist school for children and young adults with autism in Berkshire they have used Kar2ouche in a completely different way. Rachel

---

Contacts and information

http://www.immersiveeducation.eu/

Tomlin has used it to support students in science, literacy and ICT. The students work towards ASDAN qualifications. ASDAN is an awarding body that accredits skills for learning, skills for employment and skills for life. It has been especially useful in the arena of personal skills helping students understand different types of relationships. They have created social stories to support students' behavioural needs and are using Kar2ouche to help students produce evidence for their portfolio for an ASDAN qualification.

'The students like using Kar2ouche because it makes the lesson more fun,' said Rachel. 'It helps our students relate better to a social situation as they can see the characters act something out. It also helps them to understand the way others may act or what they are trying to communicate. Above all, Kar2ouche helps develop independence and this encourages them to continue with tasks that may once have been beyond them.'

Advantages of Kar2ouche

1. It makes differentiation easy.
2. It's fun, so it improves motivation because they are learning while 'playing'.
3. It's multi-sensory and can provide visual and auditory stimuli.
4. It improves sequencing skills as they work with Storyboards.
5. It improves reading skills.
6. It can help with attention deficit as children work with texts of increasing complexity.
7. It can support the needs of children with a visual impairment as the teacher can alter the font and text size.
8. It's a great literacy tool as children learn to manipulate and interpret text.
9. The sound files and recording facility let children be more independent.

Brilliant Idea 25

There's treasure in texting

SIMON **F**ITZPATRICK **REPORTS** on an interesting mobile phone treasure hunt he ran with a group of learners with disabilities at North Tyneside College.

The project ran for seven weeks and featured a series of simple questions and tasks texted to mobile phones, one per week. The 22 students had a range of disabilities including spina bifida, hydrocephalus, cerebral palsy, epilepsy, short term memory loss and visual impairment. They were divided into groups of two, three or four, to ensure an equal spread of mobile phones, and each group had a helper.

I texted questions to them and they had to carry out a task and then text the answer back to me. The questions included tasks where they had to find and talk to particular people in college, use observation skills or use the internet. For example they had to find a named member of staff and find out her birthday; they had to find the name of a particular landmark during a residential course and name the sevenwonders of the world.

If the answer was correct, I sent each correct group a number – this number was then kept and entered onto a worksheet. If the answer given was wrong, no action was taken. Usually, groups would keep sending messages until they managed to get the correct answer.

Once students arrived at seven numbers, I arranged to transmit a 'codebreaker' to allow the students to break a simple code – e.g. A=5. The first correct answer

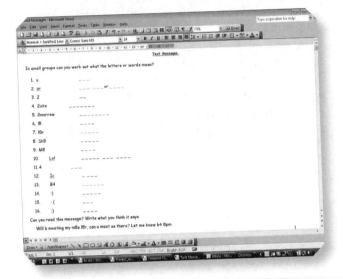

sent back to me would win a 'major' prize, although it was planned to award prizes for all correct answers.

Learning & Management issues

1. One member of the group did not take part in the exercise at all.
2. One group regularly forgot to bring their mobiles.
3. The support staff were very keen (occasionally too keen!) They certainly wanted 'their' groups to win, when they could have taken more of a back-seat role.
4. The support staff often entered the responses onto the phone keypad, where students experienced physical difficulty.

Contacts and information

SMS Poll – http://www.smspoll.net/

Poll Everywhere – http://www.polleverywhere.com/

Text Someone – http://www.textsomeone.com/

At Crossways Academy in Lewisham, London, teachers say to pupils at the end of lessons: 'You know the learning objectives; if you have suggestions on how the lesson could have been better for you, text them to this number.'

Research by children's charity NCH suggested 16% of 11 to 19 year-olds had received threatening text messages. Text Someone allows schools to fight back against this trend.

Texting can beat bullying. Text Someone gives pupils the power to report incidents of bullying, theft, crime or any unwanted behaviour in confidence, 24 hours a day, seven days a week by text message, email or voice message.

You could ...

✔ Get pupils to text questions about the set texts they are studying to each other. After they've texted replies to each other they have much more knowledge of the text and have developed their ideas

✔ Set up 'voting' web pages to run activities from mobiles. Some applications are free (so long as you are only working with a class and not huge numbers) and very easy to use. This means you can do voting even if you do not have voting sets

5. Students occasionally forgot which group they were in!
6. On a number of occasions students' mobiles had no available credit – a teacher usually stepped in.
7. Where questions were individualised, the project seemed to work more effectively as there was less risk of answers being passed on by word of mouth; but this was much more difficult to organise.

The following Literacy and Numeracy objectives were achieved:

1. Students had to use the computer at least once during the exercise.
2. Students had to use the Internet and search engines in particular.
3. Students used extensive communication skills including identification and interpretation of keywords and important points.

In general, the project was a success, enjoyed by all and with some positive learning outcomes. Most students felt that this was something different; they saw the relevance of texting and it broadened minds – some even admitted that they had learnt a lot. They appreciated being able to bring phones into class legitimately; they enjoyed receiving the messages and carrying out the research. Although only three of the group thought they had good texting skills most of them enjoyed the treasure hunt, said they had found it easy and that there had been no technical hitches.

Brilliant Idea 26

Coping With Chaos in the classroom

COPING WITH CHAOS is a story-based program about emotions and behaviour, suitable for children with emotional and behavioural difficulties. It features a child called Sam, who finds himself in a variety of difficult situations which are commonplace for most students. Rosie Murphy of Fairfield School explains how she used the program.

Initially, I set up the program on the Interactive Plasma Screen to use with a group of KS3 students. Some of these students have emotional problems, some on the autistic spectrum. The program has three levels of difficulty ranging from simple to more complex emotions. When the program starts we are introduced to Sam and he waves hello – a great touch as confirmed by my students, who enthusiastically waved back!

The program features a variety of easily recognisable locations for the students to choose from but, to avoid confusion, only two are shown on the screen at a time. Once the location has been selected something surprising happens to Sam and he expresses an emotional reaction. As one of the options, students can choose which surprise they would like Sam to receive. This is a useful tool as they can select a familiar situation, for example dropping an ice cream on the floor. At each stage in the program there is an animation of Sam which encourages the students to watch and they are unable to move to the next stage until it finishes.

Although Coping With Chaos works very well with students who can access the plasma screen by touching it, I also used the switch option with a group of KS3/4 students. The program can be accessed by either one or two switches but, to accommodate all the needs of the students in the group, the mouse or touchscreen can still be used at the same time. By setting the correct scan rate for my students, they could access the program by pressing a switch when the scan box reached the required button.

As an addition to the lesson I printed off the pictures in the 'resources' section of the program. These enabled students to look at the choices and select at their leisure before using a switch, thereby reducing the

pressure of choice making, scanning and switching at the same time. Also available are sheets for lotto boards and dominoes as well as small and large pictures of the emotions with empty speech bubbles so words can be added.

As each story is completed a star is given and the student can print out a certificate giving their score. Incorporated into the program are signs and symbols (sadly not PCS) and my students watched and signed in response. Throughout the program there is also positive reinforcement of the correct way to behave and simple explanations on why certain choices might not be appropriate. The program promoted a lot of discussion with some students and we talked about different reactions to difficult situations and what is appropriate behaviour. Overall this program was a big hit with our students. The graphics are clear and interesting. The subject matter is appropriate and it lends itself to group work on the Interactive Plasma Screen.

You could ...

✔ Use the program on an interactive whiteboard

✔ Match pictures and symbols for different emotions

✔ Use a digital camera to take pictures of pupils to illustrate different emotions

✔ Type different emotions into Google and click on Images

Contacts and information

Coping With Chaos –
    http://www.inclusive.co.uk/

Brilliant Idea 27

A little PSP goes a long way

*E*ACH *PEACH PEAR Plum* is a very popular bedtime story but at Longwill School for Deaf children in Birmingham they have created a truly individual version.

In the reception area there are puppets the children have made of Tom Thumb, Bo-Peep, Mother Hubbard and the rest of the crew. On each puppet is a little semacode marker, a type of barcode which looks like a crossword puzzle. Attached to the table by a low-tech piece of string is a Sony PlayStation Portable (PSP). Hold it so the camera scans the semacode and you will see a child signing the page in British Sign Language (BSL).

In 2007, the children in Foundation and in Year 5/6 were each given a PSP. One objective was to improve language development both in BSL and English for the younger children. By using the Second Sight Viewer (a UMD that slips into the back of the PSP) the school has built up a virtual library of signed stories that can be loaded onto the PSPs and taken home to be shared with the rest of the family. This helps hearing families improve their BSL while the children are improving their literacy. Fathers also seem to be taking more interest in homework now the children have their PSPs!

With the older group the staff wanted to develop higher-order thinking skills. Deaf children so often have to operate in English, their second language. They would ask questions and gather information but you can't sign and write at the same time. By the time they came to write up their findings the language was very simplistic and did not reflect the complexity of the discussion. Now they can film debates or, if one pupil is asking questions, another will act as cameraman. They can review the footage, rehearse their sentences in BSL and then translate them back into written English.

The PSPs have had a positive impact on spelling. In the past, children would copy words off the board while the teacher explained them in BSL. Spelling is especially hard for deaf children as they can't hear the word and often need to be told what it means as well. They used to draw sign graphics to aid recall but could not always interpret them at home. Now they stand around the interactive whiteboard where the words are written and film as the teacher explains, signs and finger spells the word. In their long journeys home, they can get out their PSPs and practise their spellings.

Now every single child at Longwill has a PSP and it is working wonders for home school links. 'Pupils find it hard to tell their parents what they're doing,' says deputy head Alison Carter. 'Now with the PSPs parents can see what we have done. Parents often film the children at home and we can watch this on the interactive whiteboard in the Monday morning news session. We have had some great moments. We saw Bryce's little brother when he was hours old and we saw Sarah's newly decorated bedroom – very pink with a purple duvet. Our children come by taxi from as far afield as Worcester and Sandwell so the children almost never go to one another's houses.' It can also help keep parents informed. One boy who has autism as well as being deaf has issues with food. His parents were very concerned and kept asking if he was eating at school. Alison filmed him lining up with the other children, getting a plate of food on his tray and eating. A 30-second clip made all the difference.

'The PSPs go everywhere with them,' said Alison. 'Initially we bought wrist straps for them to carry them around but this was a mistake because you can't sign with a PSP hanging off your wrist so now they have lanyards which go round their neck.

'They have made an incredible difference to our pupils. During the year-long trial, not one child forgot their PSP, damaged it or lost it in the whole year. That has to be some kind of a record. Since 2008, every pupil has their own PSP as a learning tool and now all of the pupils take incredible care of their devices, because they understand the value in them.'

You could ...

✔ Film local events and bring them into the classroom

✔ Get parents who speak community languages to record versions of traditional stories to bring home languages into the classroom

---

Contacts and information

http://www.connectededucation.com/images/longwill.pdf

Brilliant Idea 28

Creating a communication-friendly environment with symbols

WARWICKSHIRE AND FIFE Local Authorities have taken symbols out of special education and put them into mainstream schools. Both authorities are using symbols to support children who find language and print a problem and to develop differentiated curriculum related materials.

Fife County Council advocate using Picture Communication Symbols (PCS) symbols throughout mainstream settings. The pilot project has used Boardmaker Plus! from Mayer-Johnson to provide a consistent communication-friendly environment. It started with 11 primary schools and has grown to 104 primary schools across Fife, and is now beginning to move into secondary.

Sandra Miller, Headteacher at The Fife Assessment Centre for Communication through Technology (FACCT), explained: 'The transition from primary to secondary can be very stressful for some pupils. We have used symbols to let pupils share their worries and fears. Symbols can support pupils' communication, and also their organisational skills and recall. It can help them to access text and improve their ability to cope

Contacts and information

Why we use symbols: Independence –
   http://www.symbolsinclusionproject.org/symbols/why_symbols/independence.htm
Widgit – http://www.widgit.com/
FACCT – http://www.acipscotland.org.uk/facct.html
Mayer-Johnson: testimonials –
   http://www.mayer-johnson.co.uk/whole-school-testimonials
Boardmaker Case Study – Fife Assessment Centre for Communication Through
   Technology
http://www.youtube.com/watch?v=Hg_xy0wOPuU&feature=mfu_in_order&list=UL

with change, so you can see why we hope that more schools will adopt symbols!'

The project has made an impact. Already many secondary schools are 'symbolising' their public areas and individual teachers have received training so they now understand why symbols can be effective and can see ways they could use them in their classroom.

'Once schools are on board,' said Miller, 'they take ownership for developing symbol support and resources. This means that they can intervene and make immediate provision for a child rather than waiting for a speech and language assistant to make them two weeks later, as sometimes happened.'

Maureen Pickering, Deputy Headteacher at Benarty Primary School in Fife said, 'If children have any kind of learning need then symbols are the way forward. Schools can customise symbols for their own environment and they are so easy to use that the children can make their own visual timetables.

'Learners are using symbols from an early age and are quite used to this and the staff find the symbolising is quite addictive!'

In Warwickshire they have been using Widgit Literacy Symbols. Pauline Winter at Clapham Terrace Primary used symbol versions of 'Roman' books with a boy, who was very difficult to motivate and a girl who was Portuguese with huge gaps in English vocabulary.

'The boy loved the symbol book,' said Pauline. 'I read the first page, then he wanted to read the rest. When I paused to check the vocabulary, he impatiently said 'Let's get on. I want to read this bit. In the second

session that week both children showed continued interest, and remembered a few of the new terms introduced. In this session they used the flash cards to identify specific vocabulary and discuss the meanings. By the second week, both children had a good recall of vocabulary and good attention to the tasks. They both made a big effort to recall the labels from last time. The specific vocabulary they could recall was Rome, Emperor, sword, shield, aqueduct, legion and the purpose of turtle formation.'

'By the end of that week they were able to read from the symbol-supported books. These books have symbol/pictures linked to the new and difficult vocabulary. It was clear that the symbols helped them to remember and understand the concepts.'

Key points for symbol support

1. Teachers may not want to symbolise every word. They might just use them for key words or difficult concepts.
2. Symbols can give a voice to children who have speech language and communication needs (SLCN).
3. They can help children understand a text so they have a context for decoding words.
4. They can help with choice making activities.
5. Teachers can build a bank of differentiated resources.
6. Verbal instructions can be reinforced with a symbol card.
7. They can help pupils be more independent.

Brilliant Idea 29

Visualiser brings classwork into focus

ONE PIECE OF TECHNOLOGY can help pupils with visual impairment or dyslexia and works well for students who aren't even in school: the visualiser, a camera-come-projector capable of high-resolution output. Helen Davis (Science AST) shows how the visualiser is transforming life for teachers at Davison C of E High School for Girls in Worthing.

Before we had visualisers it was very hard work providing differentiation and meeting the needs of different pupils: large print and a special font for Natalie who has a visual impairment, photocopying handouts onto yellow paper for Beth who has specific learning difficulties (SpLD). Photocopying took up too much time and cost the school a lot of money. We also had to incorporate lots of repetition in class for children who had problems concentrating and any girl who missed a lesson would have to catch up by working from books and handouts and talking to a friend. It is a very different story now.

Science involves a fair number of demonstrations. In the past we would have had a group of girls standing in a circle round the front table. There would be lots of jostling; some would not be able to see clearly what was going on and others would walk away and soon forget the steps they had to follow to replicate the experiment. Now we use the camera on the visualiser to film what we are doing during the demonstration so it is large enough for all to see on the whiteboard screen and play it back during the practical so everyone can see what comes next. We can also keep recordings for revision and pupils enjoy making their own videos using stop frame animation. This helps them model conceptually difficult ideas and share them with a wider audience making a richer learning experience for all.

The visualiser is a wonderful tool for enlarging detailed processes. With circuit boards in design and technology, pupils need to see exactly where to apply a soldering iron but the components of a circuit board are very small. With the visualiser, we are not just helping girls to get things right, we are also keeping them safe.

Another example is the investigation into factors affecting the rate of photosynthesis, utilising aquatic plants. All green plants take carbon dioxide in and turn it into oxygen in their leaves. The key way we can measure this easily in class is to count the number of oxygen bubbles produced from a cut plant shoot in a set time period. We use Cabomba, a fluffy pond weed for the aquarium which works very effectively even with very low light levels. Often the bubbles are so small that they are hard to see with the naked eye. Now that with the visualiser they are larger and much more obvious we can also record the evidence . We know everyone is seeing the same thing now which makes for more reliability and precision.

Contacts and information
Visualiser forum – http://www.visualiserforum.co.uk/
Inclusion case studies – http://www.visualiserforum.co.uk/case-studies/sen/
AverVision – http://www.avermedia-europe.com/default.aspx
Elmo – http//www.elmo-visualiser.co.uk
GeneeWorld – http://www.geneeworld.com/
Samsung – http://www.samsungpresenter.com/
WolfVision – http://www.wolfvision.com/wolf/1.shtml

The visualiser helps us to meet individual needs within the classroom. We can put a handout on the visualiser and put a yellow acetate over the top so Beth can see it clearly. She is not being singled out and it does not affect the others in the class. We also have learners who have a good grasp of science but cannot write up their work. We can assess how much they know by letting them make posters or record them presenting to a group. This is very useful for peer and self assessment. We can also put up a good written account on the visualiser from one of the other pupils so they have a model of what they should be aiming at. Sometimes they need to see what 'good work' looks like in order to improve their own work.

Hayley has ASD and has problems interpreting pictures as do some of the girls with specific learning difficulties. Somehow they cannot see a two-dimensional image on a page and relate it to something three dimensional. When we study the differences between plant and animal cells we make cardboard models and show them on the visualiser. Somehow working in 3D lets them see the differences so much more clearly and there is less room for misinterpretation.

Because visualisers are so widely used in school lessons, we are building a bank of videos and this can be very useful when children are absent from school for long periods or who are school refusers. The children have to do some practical assessments as part of their GCSE and we give them a run through so they know what to expect.

Aisha was in hospital having operations on her knees when we did an investigation on force and momentum. We ran a model car down slopes taking very precise readings via a light gate. Instead of getting her to work from a book or copy up a friend's notes, we videoed the lesson and emailed it to her in hospital so she could understand exactly what we had done. Now she can do the paper knowing full well what is required and she has as good a chance as any of the girls who were physically present in the lesson.

Top ten tips

1. Ensure that staff and pupils are already comfortable with the existing display technology in the school (like interactive whiteboards).
2. Consider buying a visualiser with its own light source (these are more versatile – but they cost more). Nearly all of these have light source in built these days!
3. Make time to see the technology being used. Try visiting a school that already uses the technology, or ask to have training from the education consultant for the company.
4. Ask if the images/videos created by the visualiser can be shared easily. Usually, they can be saved on a laptop, on the interactive whiteboard or on an SD memory card. (This is not worth it, nearly all visualisers do this!)
5. Skill the children up. The visualiser you choose needs to be robust enough for everyday use – but it will last longer when everyone knows what they are doing!
6. Consider buying a docking station – it will allow you to shift from laptop to DVD to visualiser seamlessly.
7. Spend a little time planning when you will use your visualiser over the year (spontaneity is also good!).
8. Pair staff who are ICT literate with those who are less so to ensure consistent use within the school. Encourage teachers to share their ideas and teaching techniques (use the Visualiser forum).
9. Visualisers are like any other ICT resource. To get the most out of them, you need a plan. Used properly, visualisers mean the advantages we were promised with interactive whiteboards (increased pupil engagement, reduced preparation time, improved results) are finally realised.
10. To ensure visualisers don't just clutter your desk, you have to get the children on board. Once they have shared their work, interests and ideas on the visualiser, they won't let you forget about using it!

Brilliant Idea 30

Using a TomTom to make sense of the world

K. **C. KELLY-MARKWICK IS HEAD OF ICT** at Oakwood Court College in Devon and her work with Global Positioning Systems (GPS) won her the Handheld Learning Award for Special Needs and Inclusion 2010. This project could easily be adapted to different groups of learners in schools and helps with mobility and communication skills.

Oakwood Court College is a specialist residential educational college for 35 students with Asperger's syndrome, autism, Down's syndrome, Williams syndrome and other types of learning difficulties.

Self-reliance is a key quality that the college fosters in its learners to ensure that people with learning difficulties have the knowledge and confidence to apply for jobs and live as independently as possible when they leave college.

One project focused on a comparison of the speeds of email and conventional 'snail mail'. Students started by making their own Christmas cards on the computer and printing out a copy. They wrote the name and address – and most importantly – the postcode of the person they were sending it to on the envelope. Staff at the college explained what a postcode is and what it does. To help this process they visit the website Flash Earth and put the postcode into the satellite navigation system to see how it related to the location and postcode. A screen grab of the map was printed out and used as evidence in their folder (OCR National Skills Profile Module 1: Interact and use ICT for a purpose).

Once the students understood how the postcode works, they moved on to using the TomTom GPS system. With a bit of help from staff, the students put in the postcode for their local post office and set off on foot to find it. There they bought their stamps and posted their cards. When they arrived back at the college, the students had to send the same card to the same person via email. The students then compared how long each took to arrive.

'People think of the TomTom as a technology just for motorists,' said KC, 'but it has been an inspiration, giving the students greater independence and improving

You could ...

✔ Compare maps – printed ones, Google Earth, Google Maps

✔ Go for a walk with cameras and clipboards – take pictures and create your own map

✔ Look at Google Maps' Street View

their communication skills. It led them to go into the local community and use maps and life skills that they may not ordinarily use within a college environment.'

The satellite navigation system has been used for other outside visits so the students have started to learn about different places within their community. It also links to modules such as the OCR for Accreditation Life and Living (ALL) where they look at the use of technology in everyday life, at college and work. As they go out and about they can find out about:

1. CCTV cameras in the shops
2. ATM bank machines
3. Control panels at pelican crossings
4. Shop counter check-out points
5. Public pay phones

'The students get a greater sense of purpose from these activities,' said KC, 'and their whole experience has been enriched as a result, developing their education and practical skills.'

Contacts and information

Flash Earth – http://www.flashearth.com/

Brilliant Idea 31

Spinning a yarn: using DVDs to raise writing standards

SOMETIMES DESCRIBED AS 'the oldest art form in the world', storytelling is central to our world. We think in narrative form and relate the stories each day describing what we did at the weekend or recalling family exploits. Stories are also a traditional medium of passing knowledge on from one generation to the next and a great tool for education and therapy.

The Story Spinner project, run by the School Effectiveness Division (Curriculum Innovation) and Birmingham Library Services, aimed to improve levels of reading, writing and spoken language.

The DVDs feature stories from around the world and offer a model so teachers and children can tell stories in ways that will engage the audience's emotions and invigorate their imaginations. Teachers involved in the project reported that after experiencing Story Spinner, the structure and imaginative content of the children's told and written narratives improved noticeably over the course of one term. These gains were sustained and enhanced over time.

Some of the improvements can be seen clearly in these samples of work produced by Lucia:

You could ...

- ✔ Bring a professional storyteller into classroom
- ✔ Get children performing their own stories for parents and grandparents
- ✔ See if there are storytellers in the local community who can share tales from their culture
- ✔ Get children to retell familiar family stories
- ✔ Create animations of well known tales
- ✔ Create stories in PowerPoint or in a storyboarding package such as Kar2ouche

Example 1 – before the project – April

On sunday orlagh came over mine to sleep over We stayed up till 1.00 am in the on the psp and The ds and The computer and Hide and seek my dad

Although it fulfils the purpose asked by her teacher – to write about a holiday experience – there is little sense of awareness of the reader in this piece. The sequence is purely chronological and seemingly unselective, describing everything the girls did.

Example 2 – after the project – May

Theseus meets the minotaur

When Theseus got down the well he got his streng up to Kill the minotaur and he got worried about his father in case he never came back So any he started to make my way through the maze He was walking through for along time.

The creatures eyes where Like crimson red gem's of blood and his finger nails like crab claw. Shockingly he had horn's like daggers and the head and shoulder of a bull.

Not long after that Theseus found the minotaur and he steped forward with braveness and so did the minotaur so he took one more steps forward and ran up to the minotaur, leaped got his sword and stabd it into the minotaur's bottom

Although Lucia still has problems with spelling and punctuation, the second piece shows real development. It is more interesting and imaginative, with references to Theseus' state of mind as well as a vivid description of the Minotaur. It directly addresses the reader ('so anyway') and selects important actions by Theseus. The narrative is sequenced and structured clearly.

The vocabulary is much more adventurous than in the first example and is used effectively. For example, the placing of 'Shockingly' at the beginning of a sentence. The imagery is appropriate and telling, particularly in the middle paragraph. Again, almost all the spelling is accurate, and in this much longer piece Lucia has been successful in spelling unfamiliar words.

Why DVDs are effective

1. Parts can be repeated.
2. Teachers can review the stories before using them.
3. Children learn some of the conventions and set phrases of storytelling.
4. Listening to stories on a regular basis improves pupils' attention span.
5. It can support children who are learning English as they allow them to listen as many times as they like to the expected structures and cadences of spoken English narrative.

Contacts and information

http://thestoryspinner.co.uk/stories-from-around-the-world

Brilliant Idea 32

'Would all cashiers return to their cash desk?': ICT supporting role play

**Maggie Wagstaff,
Independent Consultant**

THE **DIY STORE** planning example shows how ICT, and in this instance maths, can be a vehicle for the development of language, social interaction and knowledge and understanding of the world. The enjoyment of real life use of technology complements the need to embed ICT across the curriculum and make learning meaningful for all children. It is so much easier to be engaged and enthusiastic if you have a role to play. Activity-based learning is often more productive and tolerant of the needs and behaviours of children with SEN and provides opportunities to take risks and experience the results of their own and other children's actions.

Some examples of the benefits

1. Children who use ICT for their communication can practise its use in situations beyond their classroom targets. **At the checkout** – programmed into children's communication aids were customer service announcements, store closing warnings, calls for different staff to come to areas of the store. Children could choose which and when to press and say.

2. The resources reflect the technology children see in the world around them and help them transfer and apply their skills and knowledge. **Security** – Phones, walkie talkies, webcams used as cctv, gave the security guards an 'important' job to do and increased self esteem and personal responsibility. Making door entry systems reminded the children about access for wheelchairs, trolleys, pushchairs, mobility scooters and those with sensory difficulties. A child with VI 'invented' automatic doors that said 'I am opening.'

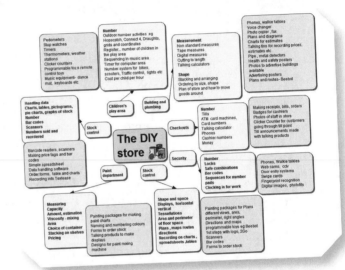

3. The open ended nature of role play nurtures creativity and demands social interaction and decision making, without the pressure of there being a right answer – the script evolves as the children play, the adults observe, facilitate and play their part too. **Paint department** – using painting packages with a purpose, to make paint charts, displaying and selling inspires children to give names to the colours, print labels and make advertising material. The displays were enhanced by using the range of reasonably priced talking products such as talktime mats, talking speech bubbles, talking pegs, postcards and photo albums; talking tins attached to a magnetic strip so that the messages recorded can be ordered and sequenced easily. The children had fun recording prices and special offers.

4. **Doing is better for remembering!** Practical tasks as described in the Building and Plumbing section allowed children to use a variety of measures according to their ability. Digital measuring devices are ideal for those with limited mobility. The arrangement of goods and store plans offers

You could ...

✔ Adapt this idea for a doctors' surgery using monitors for heart rate etc.

✔ Create a vets' clinic and link to Brilliant Idea 37

scope for children who find it difficult to relate to themselves in the space around them. Using Beebots and remote control toys is great fun for moving stock around the store. Beebot also made an excellent store stalking, undercover security guard.

5. **Repetition and rehearsal**, which ICT has traditionally, even tediously, been used for, has so much more meaning and scope for the transfer of skills, when the cashier has to use their till, calculator, card swipe machine and make calls for the supervisor, as the customers keep coming!

Timing 'work shifts' helped children take turns and was related to the planning for their day (visual timetables).

The DIY store focuses on maths and ICT but includes many other curriculum areas and is:

1. Planned to use a breadth of commonly used technology
2. Planned so that ongoing assessment and evidence of progression and achievement are a natural and integral component e.g. photos, videos, audio recordings
3. Planned to make use of curriculum software and free utilities (see hardware and software recommendations below)
4. Planned to be accessible and fun for everyone

Children's comments

'When I was the security guard I had big responsibilities.' (EBSD)

'It's funny when I made my paint chart names it wasn't like table writing.' (Global delay referring to writing in class)

'I am sure I am now qualified to get a job cutting and measuring wood it was my department you see.' (Autism)

'My paint chart was used on the big display. Not bad for Mr Messy!' (CP and VI)

'I did "store will be closing in 5 minutes". I used the voice changer so no one knew it was me!' (Speech and language difficulties)

Contacts and information

Software

Painting packages
Free painting packages to download
Tux Paint – http://www.tuxpaint.org/
Drawing for children – http://drawing.gamemaker.nl/
Kiddo – http://www.snowytree.com/kiddo/index.html
Pictogram e.g. Kudliansoft
Desktop publisher e.g. Textease
Talking faces free download from – http://www.inclusive.co.uk/downloads#talkingfaces

Hardware

Digital camera, web cam
Talking scanner/bar code reader (toy)
Tills, ATMs, talking calculator
Phones, walkie talkies
Range of low tech talking devices to include talktime mats, postcards, A4 message cards, talking speech bubbles talking photo albums, talking tins
Metal detector
Pedometer
Timers, stopwatches, counting clickers
Thermometers
Battery testers, digital measuring devices, pipe and metal detectors
Programmable toys e.g. Beebot
Power tools use with switches and power link box to operate electrical devices
Music equipment for the children's play area – dancemats, keyboards, guitars, lights fans bubble machines, sensory equipment, MP3 players, CD player

Brilliant Idea 33

Gaming is good for you!

SOME SEE COMPUTER games as a hobby: fun for an after-school club but not education. However, the Consolarium project in Scotland has been encouraging young people to become creators – not just consumers – of games. Their research has shown that games making can help pupils develop self-reliance, problem-solving and critical thinking skills.

Sheffield West City Learning Centre Manager Alex Jones shows how a group of young offenders benefited from creating their own educational games. The programme worked with two groups of young offenders who were aged 15–17 and were school refusers, excluded or being educated in Pupil Referral Units (PRUs). They had a range of learning difficulties such as ADHD, autism, behavioural disorders and Post Traumatic Stress Disorder.

The programme began with a session evaluating widely available games such as *Pro Evolution Soccer* so the participants got a sense of the kind of games that were available and what sort of games activities they liked. They then went on to create their own games using Immersive Education's *MissionMaker* programme. The software is easy to use and unlike other gaming engines, you get a professional-looking game very quickly.

The young people had to develop the game rules and scenario and choose what sort of props they would need. One game had a complicated series of moves featuring gates and locked doors which would not open unless the player had first collected a number of items from different areas.

Like most quest-type games, the players could choose weapons and this led to some pertinent discussions. Two young men had used guns in their games. One removed them from his game after a discussion with the session leader and the other removed his without being asked. They developed a policy that guns *could* be included in the game but only if they were linked to a consequence, such as being imprisoned. So the gaming opened up a good debate about the consequences of carrying weapons.

MissionMaker provided lots of opportunities for learning. The groups tested out ideas, finding out what

Contacts and information

http://www.ltscotland.org.uk/usingglowandict/gamesbasedlearning/gamedesign/index.asp

Brindley, S 'ICT and Literacy' in Gamble, N and Easingwood, N (2000) ICT and Literacy, Continuum

Scratch games creator – http://scratch.mit.edu/

Microsoft Kodu – http://research. microsoft.com/en-us/projects/kodu

2DIY – http://www.2simple.com/2diy/examples/

MissionMaker – http://www.immersiveeducation.eu/

Derek Robinson's games blog – http://hotmilkydrink.typepad.com/my_weblog/ consolarium Ideas, tips and links to resources.

Ollie Bray's website, practical advice on the use of computer games for learning – www.olliebray.com

You could ...

- ✔ Start by looking at games that pupils use at home
- ✔ Try to find examples of different types of game – action, adventure, sport, role play, strategy
- ✔ Think about ways of evaluating games
- ✔ Use it as the basis of work in design & technology and English
- ✔ Get pupils to create games for vocabulary work in MFL

worked through trial and error and by analysing their mistakes. Their finished games were of a high quality and involved complex construction.

All those who took part developed their communication skills so they could describe and discuss how they had built different aspects of the game. Behaviour was generally very good during the sessions as the groups stayed calm and on task. During lunch and refreshment breaks they were keen to return to their games.

One young man who has significant mobility problems had been out of school for a year. He was seen as being disaffected and turned off by any form of learning yet he arrived at each of the sessions on time,

coming by tram and then walking half a mile uphill to the centre. The games sessions certainly motivated him!

All those who completed the programme achieved two credits towards an ASDAN qualification. They also took part in an awards event where they had to demonstrate their game on a whiteboard in front of an audience which consisted of parents/carers, support workers and an industry representative.

The project was a partnership between Sheffield West City Learning Centre and Sheffield Youth Offending Service and between the CLC and Immersive Education. It was funded by the European Community.

Brilliant Idea 34

Using online video to bring citizenship to life

PUPILS ARE ACCUSTOMED to using social networking websites and modern technologies such as digital cameras. They expect to see these technologies in the world around them but even now the majority of school resources are paper based. Online video is a good choice for promoting debate in PSHE, RE & Citizenship

Andrea Keightley is an ICT teacher at Montsaye Community College in Northamptonshire and is a fan of TrueTube. 'The resources that are currently available on TrueTube are specifically aimed at the age group I need them for. The video clips are presented in a modern, snappy way that appeals to teenagers of all abilities. They use real people that the audience can identify with, and present a much needed reliable replacement for out-of-date resources that often represent an unrealistic picture of society today'.

Students are suddenly willing to engage with the lesson as they can relate to the people on the screen. Some of the topics covered in the Citizenship/PSHE curriculum are 'difficult' subjects to teach, they entail exploring issues that can be or have affected students in the class. TrueTube is an online collection of moderated resources, covering everything from bullying to obesity, from street crime to sexual promiscuity. Headlines reflect the variety and impact of the resources: 'Slept With 2,000 Prostitutes', 'Are Sweatshops a Necessary Evil?', 'ASBOs Infringe the Rights of Those Who are Given Them' and so on. By watching some of the clips, the issues can be discussed using other people's views and experiences and the students can be exposed to differing opinions and situations without entering the potential minefield of their own personal experiences.

TrueTube is fully moderated so students can be encouraged and directed to use the site. The clips can

be downloaded as a resource and can also be embedded into a VLE for access elsewhere. This supports both the school and the students. A teacher or student can use the clips without having to rely on an Internet connection if they have been downloaded, and, by having access to the website or the embedded clips via a VLE the students can watch clips again or explore topics further at their own convenience.

One of the more unusual and exciting features of the site as an educational resource is the ability for the students to capture and upload their own video clips. They are then able to use the online editing facilities to create a professional-looking media clip. These clips can then be submitted to the site for moderation and possible inclusion for others to view. The use of multimedia in the classroom often has the effect of stimulating interest and so can enable students who would otherwise be uninterested in the topics being taught to be involved and increase their knowledge as well as those who would normally take part.

Contacts and information

http://www.truetube.co.uk

An online video drama with lesson plans and classroom resources –
   http://www.truetube.co.uk/being-victor

What can you do other than just watching a video?

1. Look at a story and present an opposing argument.
2. Write a headline for a story.
3. Analyse the argument – how does someone build their case?
4. Imagine the interview will be on TV – write an advert for it.

For pupils who have problems with speech and language

1. First, watch silently. See if they can guess what is happening. They will be surprised how much they can understand from body language, pictures and setting.
2. Watch with sound. See if their assumptions are right.
3. Get them to note questions they have. See if others can answer them, 'Why is he angry?' or 'What time did she say she would be home?'
4. Make predictions for the next section of the show. 'What will happen next?'

Brilliant Idea 35

Resounding success: audio in the inclusive classroom

Carol Allen,
Advisory Teacher for ICT and
Special Needs in North Tyneside

C AROL HAS BEEN an 'early adapter' of every form of technology, ensuring it meets the needs of children with disabilities and learning difficulties. Here she talks about ways of exploiting sound in the inclusive classroom.

'My "mostest fav" bit of small-scale kit at the moment is the Sound Shuffle from TTS. Small, neat enough to fit in my bag when travelling from school to school and cheap enough to recommend to others, it has so many uses that it has become one of my "essentials"! It is able to take up to 4 minutes total recording time and then these can be replayed either sequentially or randomly.

'I am currently fascinated by using sound in the "inclusive classroom". Now this can be clever with podcasting and complex multimedia productions or instant and simple. In an EYFS classroom that I am currently working with, we are looking at how embedding technology within the learning environment, in addition to the teaching and learning activities, can make it accepted practice rather than a "special" event or add-on to the main life of the classroom.

'The shuffle comes with wall attachments making it ideal for adding sound or voice to wall displays; imagine young children describing their pictures and why they created them as part of an art display – how much better than their name and year group? By using two shuffles they could each choose another's work to comment on so adding peer assessment at a very early stage in an entirely appropriate format.

'In the reading corner, selected books have shuffles next to them with audio recordings of the stories so that non-readers, and/or those with language barriers or print impairments can enjoy reading independently. These can also be sent home to support families who want to read with their children, but who also have difficulties doing so. As

it is so quick to record a story, these can be changed easily to keep the engagement high.

'Meanwhile, in the storytelling hut in the outside learning area another shuffle offers a random selection of story starters, might be a character idea; a sound effect or a snippet of music; children can take it in turns to press and then "tell" a story using the stimulus that they hear. After lunch it has been quickly re-programmed to give items to be located for a "treasure hunt", such as a stone, a leaf or a stick.

'Most EYFS classrooms offer a wealth of activities and teaching areas to choose from. For one student the range of choice was overwhelming and so they always made the same choice and were reluctant to try new things. Having a selection of activities on the shuffle, including their favourite, playing randomly, they were able to independently press, listen and move to try unfamiliar activities independently. As the top of the shuffle can be removed and a photograph or symbol fixed underneath, activities can be identified clearly. Equally, tactile items could be fixed to the lid and a selection of their "properties" recorded by the children – the opportunities are endless! Well worth a try – why not have a go and see what you can do?'

You could ...

✔ Use it to make up the recorded sound clips from a story by asking pupils to find the correct character from a selection of puppets or toys

✔ Record a series of instructions to be completed by the child

✔ Record a series of story sequences to match scanned pictures from a book, in sequence and then jumbled up for the child to put in order

✔ Have a series of pictures for the child to record their own story

✔ Record a simple story book for the child to follow whilst looking at the book

✔ Record objects that a child has to find (ideal for playtimes)

✔ Record a 'consequences' style story for each child in a group to add their own element and then illustrate the completed story

✔ Make a series of activities for children to do in PE or free choice time

✔ Record children's reactions to a visit, stimulus such as a picture or texture to create a word bank of 'wow' words

Contacts and information

Information and suppliers – www.r-e-m.co.uk and www.tts-group.co.uk

Brilliant Idea 36

Dawn of the machines

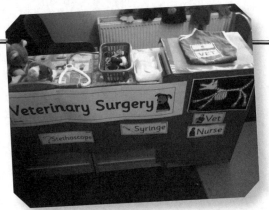

DAWN HALLYBONE IS a well known name in the world of educational gaming. A recent convert to consoles and PSPs, she is ICT Co-ordinator at Oakdale Junior School in the London Borough of Redbridge and a founder member of the Redbridge Games Network. She won the Hand Held Learning 2009 Special Achievement Awards.

'Children play games all the time. We learn through play when we are babies. So many social skills and rules for behaviour are learnt in the playground but that all goes when we move into school. I wasn't a gamer till three years ago. I didn't own a console and when my daughter, then aged 6, asked for a Nintendo DS I said no.'

But then Dawn heard about the Consolarium project in Scotland, which was bringing computer games into the classroom. This project had shown that games could help pupils develop self-reliance, problem-solving and critical thinking skills and create shared social contexts where learners could relate better to others.

Dawn introduced 30 Nintendo DS Lites into the school and found that pupils and teachers quickly became more ICT confident and more ICT literate. They discussed problems and issues together and children who had consoles at home shared their expertise with teachers and others in the class. It also led to lots of writing. The school set up a blog where the children wrote about the games they were playing at home. They also designed their own games, wrote reviews and made films about the games. They didn't just play: they worked very hard too!

Games also give us an insight into children's skills. Pupils with special needs often have low-level reading skills and are judged on that, but in fact they may have sophisticated thinking skills which we never uncover by conventional means. They may well have a high degree of media literacy and it is up to us as professionals to engage that through play. Games can provide a visual stimulus for writing. Take the Land of Me which is just beautiful. It is an old style picture book, brought to life in a different way; pupils respond to the graphics and we can use this as the basis for communication at all different levels.

Games can bring in a good element of competition. This is not the sort of competition where pupils with special needs compete against others and constantly come last but where they strive to better their own performance. For example, with Word Coach they are competing against themselves, trying to improve their spelling scores. Doing Dr Kawashima's maths on a Nintendo beats pen and paper activities hands down and it certainly encourages speed and mental agility.

For many children with dyspraxia or physical disabilities, the (Nintendo) Wii can bring a new dimension to physiotherapy. Instead of being singled out to leave the classroom, they can play on Wii Fit with a friend for 15 minutes and do their exercises in a fun way.

Good teachers use good tools and games can be very good tools indeed.

Games across the curriculum

Alissa Chesters, ICT Coordinator, has been using games with children at Oakdale Infants School. Nintendogs is a game where children look after virtual dogs. They have to feed the dog and can take him to the park, buy toys, teach him commands such as 'sit' or 'stay'. All this takes place in an online world and children use the Nintendo DS screen and a microphone. They choose a name for their dog at the beginning of the game and call their dog via the microphone. They might play on their own with the dog or link up other players using a wireless linkup. The game has an internal clock and calendar so if they don't feed and exercise their dog regularly, they see the consequences.

The school developed lesson plans and a topic web and the game was the catalyst for work in many areas of the curriculum. They had to keep the Nintendogs diary up to date so they spent at least 10-15 mins writing each day for literacy. For non-fiction they wrote up a day in the life of an RSPCA officer. They had a video of Crufts and themed their sports day as crufts4kids. In D&T they had to design a kennel and for Science they looked at what they needed to look after their dog and to keep it healthy.

You could ...

✔ Use games to inspire pupils to better their own scores and keep a chart to record improvement

✔ Use a bank of carefully chosen games or technologies as an overlearning or repetition tool

✔ Ask pupils to record on a sound shuffle or Easi-Speak mic the rules to their games for others to follow

✔ Make a database of good games for pupils to search through and find the appropriate resource

✔ Make posters about their favourite game

✔ Use games as a stimulus for writing, i.e. create a life for your Nintendog

Remember

1. Games enable teachers to see what the learner can do.
2. Find teachers in other schools and piggyback off their expertise.
3. Share resources and ideas.
4. With games the teacher is not in charge: some children will know more so you need an environment where it is acceptable to share knowledge.
5. Do not confine the use of games to 'golden time'.
6. Look at ways of using games on interactive whiteboards as the basis of whole class activities.

Contacts and information

Trailblazers recognised at Handheld Awards – http://tinyurl.com/652kf9b

Consolarium – http://www.ltscotland.org.uk/usingglowandict/gamesbasedlearning/consolarium.asp

FutureLab – http://www.ltscotland.org.uk/Images/futurelabgames_and_learning_tcm4-452087.pdf

Brilliant Idea 37

Lights, action, sing karaoke?

KARAOKE MACHINES HAVE been around for a long time but now there are a range of relatively cheap chidren's karaoke machines and packs to use on the computer that can be projected onto a bigger screen to enable groups of children to access them. Music and singing is a great way to overcome confidence, fluency, stammering and presentation difficulties. Many special schools use music to overcome speech and language difficulties.

Nathan Cresswell of Pioneer School in Basildon listed the numerous ways in which singing to a karaoke machine helped those children who otherwise found it difficult to communicate.

'We have used karaoke as a way to encourage confidence, listening and performance skills, especially those who choose not to speak for a variety of reasons,' he said. 'These can range from elective mutes to crippling shyness. We have also found that singing along to a familiar song helps stammerers and those with enunciation difficulties.'

Nathan chose to use a karaoke pack on the computer linked to an overhead projector to allow children to deliver and perform songs in assemblies as well as special events.

'We found that the correct microphone was essential to the success of the delivery. The lapel microphones or head mics (Madonna mics) allowed students to focus on the highlighted words and concentrate on the performance rather than the hand-held microphones, which tend to get in the way of what we were trying to achieve.'

He often uses music and singing at the beginning or end of a session but stresses that good visuals and clear text are very important, as is the colour of the highlighter that pin points the words being sung.

'We had a young lad called Paul who was 14 and had chosen not to speak. He really couldn't see any need to voice any requests and consequently found it difficult to enunciate any essential requests that he might have. Paul loved our karaoke sessions and would light up when the time came to sing along with everyone else. It really gave him a purpose to speak and sing and obviously enjoyed the activity. His favourite selection was Beatles songs!'

As well as the benefits gained from using their voices and practising hard-to-pronounce vocabulary, other side benefits came from an increase of confidence, self esteem and the social skills needed to take turns. Singing often brings joy not only to those taking part but also to those listening – it takes the stress away from essential speech therapy practice and injects a wonderful sense of fun.

For a price of around £15 for a karaoke pack this is a fantastic tool for all children.

You could ...

✔ Sing your favourite songs at the end of the day
✔ Hold your own X-Factor
✔ Hold your own karaoke disco
✔ Practice favourite songs for delivery in assemblies or school productions
✔ Make up your own pantomime including the songs
✔ Just have fun!

Extra information

Stand-alone karaoke machines for children start at about £50 – http://www.argos.com

Karaoke packs for use on your computer start at about £15 – http://www.argos.com

Just Dance on the Wii contains an element of karaoke along with dance moves for £15 – www.amazon.co.uk

Sing to the world is a karaoke website where, for a subscription of £6.99 per month, you can get unlimited access to a huge database of songs – http://www.singtotheworld.com

Brilliant Idea 38

Accessible music in a cube

YOU MAY NOT have heard of the Skoog yet, but you soon will. It is a white squeezy cube with colourful curved discs on five sides which let very severely disabled children make music for themselves. Usually musical notes are dictated by the size and shape of the instrument which makes them. A recorder needs to be hollow and have holes which can be covered up to change the pitch but the Skoog lets children play 12 instruments including the piano, flute, guitar, drums and marimba. More than that, it can be programmed with any sampled sound, a song, a sound effect or will launch a midi device or a program such as GarageBand.

Pioneered at Edinburgh University with experts in music, physics and psychology working together, it can be configured to suit individual needs. It can be made sensitive to the slightest touch to encourage children to engage in cause and effect activities. The Skoog acts as a sensor and links to software which does all the hard work of making music so children who do not have the physical dexterity to play a guitar, who cannot control their breathing to play a flute can still make music for themselves.

They have been trialling it with children who have severe disabilities including sight loss. Rhys is 4 ½ and has nystagmus, photophobia, autism and global developmental delay. It worked well for his hand and eye coordination and his gross motor skills. In fact he played the Skoog with hands, feet, knees, elbows, head and chin. He also crawled through the play tunnel while playing it and ventured up the climbing frame. He expressed his opinions and told us that the instruments he preferred were the drums, guitars, xylophone, drag n' drop playthrough and sampler. Staff reported that he played for a very long time (unusual for him) and showed unexpected inventiveness, using various parts of his body to make music.

Cameron is the same age as Rhys and has a similar range of disabilities. His hand/eye coordination was good enough to control the Skoog easily, so staff turned the sensitivity down to make it more of a challenge for him. He loved hearing different instruments and realised he could make long notes rather than short ones. Usually Cameron has a very short attention span and he did walk away twice but chose to come back and try again. Staff were very impressed with how long he played with the Skoog and he certainly had lots of fun.

Other uses ...

✔ The instrumental service in Orkney is using the Skoog for instrumental tuition

✔ At SENS Scotland, the Skoog supports inclusive music making for a wide range ages and abilities

✔ Use the sampling functions and sound effects for storytelling

✔ Fife's Digital Literacy Creativity Team has used Skoog for digital soundtrack music

Contacts and information
www.skoogmusic.com/
Use YouTube to find videos

Brilliant Idea 39

PowerPoint and the hungry caterpillar

MOST STAFF IN schools have been 'PowerPointed to death' at some point in their career, but don't underestimate the power of this program. PowerPoint is much more than a presentation tool, especially when we let children loose on it. It can be a preparation for using other technology too.

Mandy Nelms teaches at Priorslee Primary School in Telford. She had been teaching French for two terms to a mixed ability class of Year 3 and 4 children. 'In the summer term I was looking to do something a bit different which would be fun but would also revisit and reinforce the vocabulary the children had already learnt. By sheer fluke, I came across *The Very Hungry Caterpillar* in French, or *La Chenille qui Fait des Trous* as we learnt to call it. It was ideal for my purposes as it tied in with all the work we had already done: days of the week, numbers up to 10 and food. It is one of the key books we use in reception because it has simple colourful graphics, lots of repetition and language patterns and I felt the same principles could be applied in French. If it worked well in a first language, it would also help children trying to acquire the rudiments of another language.

'Page by page I read the story to them in French and one of the classes read the English version. We compared the order of words, picked out words we already knew and guessed some of the unfamiliar words. I gave the children the task of creating their own *Hungry Caterpillar* book. Some chose to use paper and pencil crayons while others wanted to use ICT. I suggested PowerPoint because it is so easy to import graphics into the slides and also very simple to resize images and I knew we would want to make the caterpillar grow! It was easy to put in some French text too.

'Some of the lower ability children just put in the number and the name of the fruit but the more able

Le mardi elle croquet dans deux poires.

used an English/French dictionary to check the meanings of unfamiliar words and composed some simple sentences. The children could either use clip art or search online for suitable pictures. I used mixed-ability pairings for most of the tasks. While some children were very good at the language they did not really have a good eye for visual work and other children were more confident using ICT but were not so keen on writing. When the PowerPoint was finished, they shared it with Years 1 and 2, reading out the French to the younger children. What did technology add? It made the whole process so visual and kinaesthetic so it worked for children who prefer different learning styles. By working with text, pictures and sound they learnt the vocabulary and it became embedded in their long-term memory.'

'This was such a successful and enjoyable project, that a year later I repeated it with another class and this time we created an animated version. The children used Plasticine to make models of the fruit and we tried to create scenery which was as close as possible to the illustrations in Eric Carle's book. Pupils used "stop and shoot" for the animation. They took ten pictures,

Contacts and information

The Very Hungry Caterpillar and other French stories including comic books for young starters – http://www.earlystart.co.uk

A wealth of children language books and activities – www.amazon.co.uk

A wealth of language acquisition materials for many many languages including Hindi, Croatian and many more – www.little-linguist.co.uk

You could ...

✔ Use the visualiser to share the book with the class, annotate and snap shot pages

✔ Scan in the illustrations to put into IWB software and annotate, sequence or use for matching activities

✔ Make games cards and posters using the illustrations and ideas from the books

✔ Use the extensive range of 2Simple software such as 2Publish or 2Create to reproduce a story or make their own language book for others to read

✔ Liven up your PowerPoint presentations with custom animation (instructions in the Brilliant Starters section) to make the characters move!

moved the models and then took ten more. They soon discovered that it was far easier to move the scenery than the Plasticine figures! One boy on the autistic spectrum loved this part. The regimentation of the process seemed to appeal to him. Finally, they checked timings and tried out the animation before adding a sound track, with different pupils narrating what the caterpillar ate on different days.

I will use the same techniques again. I have just discovered Rainbow Fish, *Arc-en-ciel le Plus Beau Poisson des Océans,* and this time we will focus on colours.'

Brilliant Idea 40

Fizzing along with the all-singing, all-dancing classroom PC

COMPUTERS ARE BECOMING more singing and dancing these days with built-in cameras and a host of extra tools. But how well do they meet the needs of children with special needs or who need extra support? Enter the Fizzbook Spin.

St Matthew Academy in Lewisham was the setting for the launch of the Fizzbook Spin 10.1 classmate PC last year. The Fizzbook is a netbook, an e-reader and a touchscreen tablet all rolled into one and it even has an inbuilt camera. The technology is a collaboration between Intel and Steljes so the machines have SMART Sync classroom management software. Linked to a wireless network, it means the teacher can see at a glance who is doing what on their machines. Pupils can vote, engage in individual work, produce drawings and text and the teacher at the front can keep an eye on the class and see those who might need extra support.

The Fizzbook has some innovative smart tools too: use the magic pen to draw a circle and you get a spotlight, draw a square around part of the content and it automatically zooms in. Pupils can use a stylus which certainly encourages better handwriting and drawing, or they can use a finger if they do not have good fine motor skills. It's rugged too, so will withstand rough treatment from the clumsiest child and is nice and light so it will not weigh down fragile children.

I watched a lesson at St Matthew where the teacher used a Soulja Boy video as a stimulus piece for work on wealth. The pupils enjoyed working two to a machine and the technology ensured that the lesson went at quite a fast pace as they were all kept on task. The school likes the fact that Fizzbook fits in a school bag and doesn't take up the whole school desk. St Matthew is an academy specialising in social enterprise so the

pupils need to be able to record their activities and achievements on the school's software to build up their employability profile. The Fizzbooks can go out and about with them when they are engaged in community ventures too.

David Vernon, a teacher at Broadgreen Primary School in Liverpool, has been leading a KS2 project putting Fizzbooks through their paces. They have found that the Fizzbook has changed the way they work. They have moved from knowledge-based to enquiry-based learning and have found lots of different uses. They are sending emails to a French school in Ley and are exchanging information, using Google Translate to extend their language skills. They have been involved in a bedtime story project and will be donning pyjamas and taking their Fizzbook down to reception to share their stories with their buddies over a cup of hot chocolate.

Contacts and information

http://www.steljes.com
http://www.fizzbook.com

David Vernon said: 'It is important to us that pupils have access to information quickly and at any time they need it. Ultimately, having immediate access to ICT as we do now with the Fizzbooks has enabled us to develop our curriculum in this way.

'Using the Fizzbooks has impacted hugely on those pupils with SEN. Often, in terms of literacy at least, it's the physical process of picking up a pen and writing that causes most distress and problems for pupils who have learning difficulties. I realise this is over-simplifying this complex area but removing the requirement to 'write it down' appears to take away much stress for children with SEN.

'Having SEN does not preclude pupils from having fantastic ideas. But asking them to write down these ideas, in many cases, takes up nearly all their cognitive processing power to the detriment of their great ideas.

'Using a computer removes the stigma attached to other pupils and their teacher seeing their ideas written down. If it's on a screen their ideas can be easily edited and improved so they can take pride in the final piece of work.'

One of the pupils, Sam, is a Fizzbook fan too: 'I think they are great. They really helped me to do lots of new things. I also dropped one and it was fine.'

Now, you can't say that about many machines.

You could ...

- ✔ Set interactive quizzes for pupils to research and record their information for the teacher and class to review
- ✔ Create presentations for pupils to share with their classmates or another audience
- ✔ Use the touch screen to make ordering and drag-and-drop activities, as well as researching, easier
- ✔ Cause and effect programs work well on the Fizzbook for pupils with SEN but for more able students multiple choice activities work well
- ✔ Make a multi-choice book to share with pupils; pupils have to track through the book making choices. This could be a great PSHE activity about making the right choices

Brilliant Idea 41

Teddy and the toolkit

Janice Wilson teaches at Astley Park School in Chorley. The school was originally for children with moderate learning difficulties but now caters for children aged 4-16 with a range of conditions including Autistic Spectrum Disorder (ASD) and severe learning difficulties. Here she talks about what the program brings to her lessons:

'I have used My Modelling Toolkit across both key stages. I have used it with upper juniors to develop road safety. The program is a good introduction as it allows them to walk down a road, spotting hazards, before they go out on a real road. The pack comes with several follow-up activities. In KS1, they have used Make a Creature to design their own monsters. They print out their creations and write about them. We can talk about how many legs, how many eyes the creature has, and they can use words or symbols in their answers.

'Design a Bedroom is a fun choice. We use this for design and technology. They can decide whether they want a single bed or bunk beds, choose their curtains and furnishings. These might be masculine prints or girly and pink and then they can add accessories – posters, a goldfish bowl, television or computer. We use Smart Notebook software or Clicker Paint to design our own wallpaper using the different pens and special effects. Then we make 3D models. We use real wallpaper and carpet samples for this. In a similar vein, we use Create a Scene to make a playground. You start with a blank canvas and then bring in the elements they want: a swing, a sandpit, a see-saw.

'Probably the best activity for our learners is Find Teddy. This brings in so many different elements. The program hides a teddy somewhere in the scene and the children have to guess where he is. We use this with PECS boards (Picture Exchange Communication System) which have the appropriate symbols for them

SOME LEARNERS ARE not naturally adventurous. Maybe they are over anxious or over protected. Modelling offers a safe environment for a 'try it and see' approach. It also lets pupils enter other worlds and try different roles as a designer or a commentator.

The QCA Scheme of Work describes modelling as 'using a computer to explore real or fantasy situations'. Pupils understand that the representation is not an exact replica of the original. They discuss the main differences and similarities between a representation and the original. They create their own representations of real or imagined situations. For many pupils with special needs, modelling gives them a virtual version of an experience which perhaps they cannot enjoy in real life. The real versus fantasy element may not be as important for these learners as the chance to be in control for once, to make decisions and see the consequences of the choices they make.

You could ...

✔ Try online simulations – http://www.clusterweb.org.uk/Kentict/Kentict_soft_simul.cfm

✔ Look out for science simulations and recycling

to build up their comments on a sentence strip. We start with the symbol for 'I think' then add the teddy symbol. All their guesses use prepositions: in the wardrobe, under the bed, on the shelf.

'After each child has discussed where they think teddy is hiding using their sentence strips, they are given the opportunity to touch that area on the interactive whiteboard to reveal if they are correct. If their guess is right the teddy will be revealed and the game will start again. If they are wrong they are given a further opportunity to create a new sentence by guessing again. They are building cognition and practising language and sentence structures too.

'Of course we do the same activities in class with a real teddy, putting him in a box under a table but the computer version works better for some of our learners. Perhaps it is because it is so big and bright on the interactive whiteboard. Jamie has ASD and when we do the classroom activities he quickly loses interest and gives us a partial answer ('under rug') but when we use the computer version he uses the PECS strip and gets really excited making and sharing his sentences. His interest will sometimes last for up to 10 minutes.

'My Modelling Toolkit is a lovely program to use on interactive whiteboards. I use it a lot because it is visually attractive and not too over stimulating to look at. It works well for our learners because it is nice and simple, not all bells, whistles and visual distractions!'

Contacts and information
http://shop.sherston.com/sherston/

Brilliant Idea 42

The crazy gerbil

AT WESTFIELD ARTS COLLEGE in Weymouth, they use ICT across the curriculum to make their children as independent as possible. 'I want our pupils to be actively engaged in using a whole range of software to create their own animations, videos and learning resources,' said Yvonne Aylott, head of ICT. 'If they can't actually write things they can record their voice, they can make videos or take photographs. ICT can be very liberating and motivating. It lets us meet the same learning objectives in different ways which the children find more accessible.'

The school caters for pupils with moderate learning difficulties, many of whom have autism and/or complex needs and also supports pupils in a number of mainstream schools across Dorset. Two pieces of software have been especially good for their learners. Voki is a free online service that lets you make your very own talking avatar and Crazy Talk a facial animation program which will animate any photo or image so that the lips move and the character appears to speak a typed script or recorded voice.

Year 9 pupils were working on self portraits. They chose photographs of themselves or did drawings and used them as models for Crazy Talk. Once the face is loaded into the program they decide what they want their character to say: 'I was drawn by James. He found it hard to do my eyes,' 'I think my ears look big in this picture'. If they prefer, they can record their speech and attach it to the character. 'It is surprisingly realistic,' said Yvonne, 'because even when the character is not speaking, they are moving and there is a certain amount

You could ...

✔ Animate products to create adverts

✔ Have animated talking faces at the top of a worksheet to explain the task

✔ Use animated talking objects to explain a history topic such as how to make a mummy

✔ Make speaking and listening tasks to be followed by the children

✔ Make speaking faces or objects to be included in school webpages

✔ Create a play with a series of talking characters. This is a great way to introduce spoken versus written language and play script format

✔ Make a storyboard for a film or story and create characters ready to animate. Look at www.creaturecomforts.tv/uk/ for some trailers and ideas for creating animations

✔ Ask children to record and animate their thoughts on some artwork, book, poem, play or television programme and leave on the IWB for pupils to listen to

of noise (background animation), as if they are just pausing for breath. It is quite motivating for our learners. We had one boy who did not speak willingly but was really trying to make some noise so that his self portrait would not be silent. This project was good because it let the pupils think and talk about what they had done whereas they would find it hard to write an evaluation.' The pupils have found some creative uses for the software. They have made some talking trees and when they were having school council elections they animated a cow pat who did a rousing speech along the lines of, 'Vote for me. I'm so soft and squidgy!'

With Voki the children select a background such as a city at night or a harbour, choose a character, change the hair and features, add some accessories such as moustaches and sun glasses, type in some text or record a message and the character speaks. 'We used this to create some jingles for a charity campaign,' said Yvonne. 'We had an Elvis type avatar and it was just so easy to create.'

Using animated faces is obviously great fun but Yvonne warns that it is important to have some structure not just play around with it, 'The technology is not that important, it is the uses we make of it that matter. We did some work using photos of the class gerbil and then recorded a script so that the gerbil spoke and told people what it needed: 'I need clean water,' 'I like something to chew.' Children with autism can have problems with empathy but when children are devising their script, they are in fact thinking about that other person or animal and that is a good first step to thinking about others' feelings.'

Contacts and information

http://www.voki.com/
http://www.reallusion.com/crazytalk/

Brilliant Idea 43

Meeting all a pupil's writing needs

MOST WORD PROCESSORS are designed for those who can already read and write. But for those who need help to access a computer or who have difficulty with writing, tools such as onscreen keyboards, word prediction, vocabulary grids and speech can make all the difference.

WriteOnline is an online word processor with a wide range of facilities which will benefit different groups of pupils. Those with dyslexia might profit from the WorkSpace, a visual mind-mapping tool that enables pupils to organise their thoughts and ideas into mind maps before they begin to write. Some learners with limited motor skills will need to use an on-screen keyboard via a mouse or tracker ball and for those who cannot click a mouse button, the Mouse Dwell option enables them to enter text just by hovering over the required cell.

Staff at The Old Railway School in Ashford, Kent have used the program with Grace, a Year 5 pupil who has muscular dystrophy and accesses WriteOnline using

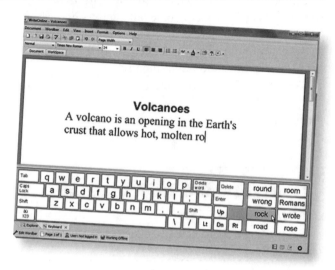

a USB Glidepoint Touchpad. Sheryl Bunyard, West Kent Communication Access Pilot Specialist Teacher said, 'Grace uses WriteOnline in most lessons; she is such a bright girl and with the support of this program

Key features

✔ Good speech which sounds as if the text is being spoken by a real human being. The speech software means pupils can hear what they have written, but also listen to words in the Wordbar grid and word predictor before writing them.

✔ Document analysis lets teachers see if work has been pasted into a text. They can also tell which spellings have been corrected by the spell checker so they can identify which words cause problems for individual learners

✔ The predictive facility lets pupils access crucial vocabulary in all subject areas. For instance, difficult vocabulary in science can be included

✔ Teachers' comments can be embedded in the text without that 'red pen' effect

✔ If the mind map facility is used then the vocabulary included in that is sent automatically into the word grid for pupils to use independently

she can really demonstrate her understanding and learning. I have been incredibly pleased with the progress that she has made using the program. She has found WriteOnline really easy to use and has learnt how to use it very quickly. Grace finds the word prediction and word banks very useful! We can create the vocabulary and phrases she needs very quickly and her writing speed is improving all the time.'

'I felt that Grace would benefit even more from WriteOnline if it included an on-screen high-frequency-letter keyboard option, with the word prediction tool on the left-hand side. This on-screen keyboard option, with all the key components required for her writing, would be grouped in one place and would let her access them with minimum movement. I contacted Crick Software and they worked with me to create one; this now comes with the program as standard!'

'When Grace is using WriteOnline in school, none of her fellow classmates bat an eyelid. This is because the program looks similar to Microsoft Word, has a familiar layout and can be used unobtrusively. The program supports her in all the right ways and she does not feel self-conscious using it among her peers. I have been very impressed with WriteOnline and the differences it has made to my pupil's daily school life. When she moves up to secondary school she will continue to use this excellent program to support her learning.'

'WriteOnline has now been integrated with Moodle and so when Grace moves onto secondary school she may well be able to pick up work that teachers have set, get going with WriteOnline and then post it back into the Virtual Learning Environment (VLE) when she has finished.'

Contacts and information

www.cricksoft.com/uk/writeonline/

Brilliant Idea 44

Switch it up: toys with a twist

CHILDREN WITH DISABILITIES can be restricted in how they learn through play. They may struggle to use traditional toys, to make marks with crayons or to join in with sand and water play. An innovative project in Norfolk is examining an alternative approach.

More than 1500 children at 50 Early Years settings in Norfolk have had a great time playing with lots of new toys, but these are toys with a difference – switch toys and games software specially suited to children with disabilities or speech and language delay or sensory impairments. The Norfolk Play AT IT Project is a joint project between Norfolk County Council which provided each setting with £2500 of equipment and Access Through Technology (ATT), a council-funded service which provided training.

The nurseries, pre-schools and children's centres were given PCs with touch screens which can be raised, lowered or angled so they are easily seen by children in wheelchairs or who are sitting on the floor. The hardware can be accessed via special keyboards with colourful chunky keys and colour-coded mice. They also received toys, such as teddy bears that speak and move at the touch of a large switch, microphones, digital cameras suitable for young children and talking photo albums.

The Clare School in Norwich caters for 95 children aged three to 19 years with physical and sensory needs. Many pupils also have complex medical and learning needs. Sarah Melton runs a class for nursery, reception and Year 1 children with 11 pupils and three Specialist Support Assistants. They received over £2,500 worth of kit, including a OneTouch touchscreen computer with a range of cause and effect software from Inclusive Technology, a BIGmack and a LITTLEmack switch, a range of switch adapted toys, talking photo albums, a Tuff Cam video camera, and a microphone.

Jamie is in Year 1 at the Clare School. He has Williams syndrome, which causes learning difficulties, developmental delay and impaired language abilities. In addition he also has some sensitivity to sound. Jamie is a happy little boy who knows what he wants and he likes to work to his own agenda. He loves music and singing and toys which he can spin and make sounds.

He now has access to a BIGmack which makes sounds when he presses it. He uses it for morning routines and can respond when the class says 'good morning'. He started using two switches with symbol grids to make choices. He took to it very quickly so Sarah decided to move him on to the Picture Exchange Communication System (PECS) and he is doing well with this. Because of the project, Sarah and her team have been able to enhance his communication skills and he is progressing very well. He is beginning to make choices and communicating his wants and needs and they would like to continue with this.

Now Jamie is using a touch screen computer and Target and Touch: Patterns software. He likes to share these with an adult and will reach out for an adult hand to start the visual and audio response. Now, with the right encouragement, he is beginning to operate the program independently and takes great pleasure in doing so. It is also hoped that control over his environment may have an effect on his communication and behaviour.

Why give these children technology rather than conventional toys? Anna James, Norfolk County Council's ATT Team Leader said: 'Technology can overcome some of these difficulties and provide alternative ways for young people to explore and interact with the world around them. It is hoped that this early intervention project will have significant results for children, not only over the next year, but well beyond that.

'It will not only support their transition to school but also help unlock the world around them.'

This case study was originally part of a longer article in *Special Children* magazine, Issue 199, February 2011 and is reproduced by kind permission of Optimus Education, www.optimus-education.com.

Contacts and information

Play AT IT Project – http://www.norfolkprepared.gov.uk/Consumption/groups/public/ documents/article/ncc083494.doc

Abilitynet Play AT IT Project – http://www.abilitynet.org.uk/play/

All the equipment was provided through Inclusive Technology – http://www.inclusive. co.uk/news/norfolk-play-at-it-all

Brilliant Idea 45

Makeover makes learning more active

THEY LIKE GETTING things done at Brentwood Special School in Altrincham Cheshire. ITV's *60 Minute Makeover* team were called in by Bev Callard, better known as Liz MacDonald from *Coronation Street*, to transform four indoor and two outdoor areas to create attractive spaces for pupils to learn and play and for the staff to relax and they managed to finish the job in just one hour. These improvements were topped up by some new technology from Promethean.

Brentwood School teaches students aged between 11–19 years with special needs and severe learning difficulties. Some also have physical disabilities and the school is keen to ensure that lessons engage, enrich and stimulate all learners. One of the improvements they made was to create a 'sensory theatre' within an existing classroom and brought in a height adjustable ActivBoard+2 with accompanying software, an ActivWand, and ActiVote Learner Response System.

Cathy Graves, Deputy Headteacher and ICT Co-ordinator at Brentwood Special School said, 'The ActivBoard+2 lets all students take part in lessons. As the board can be lowered, it is accessible to students in wheelchairs and can even be used by pupils when sitting on the floor.'

The school needs to find software which is age appropriate but simple enough to be used by pupils who are working well below their chronological age. The ActivInspire software lets teachers incorporate

Contacts and information

Trailblazers recognised at Handheld Awards – http://tinyurl.com/652kf9b

Consolarium – http://www.ltscotland.org.uk/usingglowandict/gamesbasedlearning/consolarium.asp

FutureLab – http://www.ltscotland.org.uk/Images/futurelabgames_and_learning_tcm4-452087.pdf

sound files, videos, images to get their message across. Cathy explained: 'The majority of our learners have a very short attention span, so group-based activities can often be unrewarding. Using the board and interactive software, however, lessons are much more engaging. With the primary interface, the bright, colourful tools really appeal to learners, so they are keen to take part in lessons. It can also help with their physical development as the ActivBoard provides a large space for pupils to write or draw, enabling them to use a full range of movements which can help with gross motor skills while the ActivPen requires smaller, more precise movements calling on fine motor skills. Also, because students need to take it in turns to use the pen, it helps them build key social skills in turn taking, negotiation and collaboration,' added Cathy.

But one of the best features is the voting system,. The teacher puts a question to the class and students can respond just by pressing a button on their individual keypad. This means that the teacher can find out how a class is feeling about a particular lesson topic, assess the group's understanding, or track the progress of individuals. It gives pupils the opportunity to make choices and to record their decisions quickly which is a boon for those with short term memory issues. 'ActiVote has transformed the way we conduct lessons and has made discussion sessions much more beneficial for students,' added Cathy. 'Previously, if asked a question, students would repeat the answer of another pupil. With ActiVote however, they can respond with confidence and give a more honest answer.'

You could use voting technologies ...

✔ For quizzes or multiple choice questions

✔ For identifying the correct picture or word from a selection on the screen

✔ As a means to identify how a child feels from a selection on screen

✔ As a means to identify class opinion on a particular issue

✔ As formative assessment at the beginning of a lesson and again at the end for a summative assessment

✔ As a vehicle for estimation...is it more than ? or less than?

✔ For listening activities i.e. which animal makes this noise

✔ For listening to a series of instructions and then identifying the shape or object

Brilliant Idea 46

A picture is worth so much more than a thousand words

Sue Stevens,
Teacher at Royal School for the
Deaf in Derby and ICT trainer

Alex
Funny boy
He good play football
He was good friend and kind share sweets.
He happy and smile
He looked after me when I was sick.
He got nice hair and make me laugh.

MANY PEOPLE NOW buy a computer because they want to work with images: digital photographs or video clips, scanned images, animations, clip art or Internet images. The ease with which we can now take and access still and moving images is what makes digital photography a very significant tool for hearing impaired children who often learn in a visual way.

Images can give deaf and hearing impaired children the hooks upon which to hang their learning, something concrete and more accessible than the spoken word or text that needs careful reading or translation into British Sign Language (BSL). Hard to explain concepts such as solids in science can be taught more memorably through a presentation showing solids, liquids and gases. Likewise, an Internet animation demonstrating the movement of blood around the body can speed up the learning process and put things into the correct context.

Screen based resources can be motivating and provide a more visual way to develop vocabulary in English or another language. A link can be created from an area of a picture, such as an area of a garden lawn, to another slide that clearly gives the vocabulary. When the child clicks on the lawn the presentation jumps to the slide with the correct French vocabulary. Magic!

Photographs of Warwick Castle prompted conversations about fortifications, war and how towns have defended themselves at different times. The children were able to combine their experience of a visit with an investigation of the architectural features that kept people safe. The photographs led naturally to why and because questions and also encouraged them to guess some of the answers.

A lovely use of a digital camera is to get children to take photographs of each other and to create a Positive Images Wall. The addition of text boxes around each photograph allows for text to be added on screen or written on a print out and everyone has to write something nice about that person. This can be used in PSHE but also works well as a positive reinforcement for pupils with behavioural difficulties who feel nobody likes them.

Use PowerPoint with digital images to create resources to teach grammar: a series of photos of a familiar toy can teach prepositions: the dog is on the shelf, in the slipper, behind the book, under the table. It can be printed as a book, or used on screen where children see the image and predict the text that will appear on a mouse click using the

Contacts and information

http://www.batod.org.uk/
http://www.rnid.org.uk/othersites/
Photo Story – http://www.windowsphotostory.com/ and select download

You could ...

✔ Take pictures of the school Sports Day or a visit to a museum. Use for individual work and discussion to make sure vocabulary has been assimilated and that children have grasped concepts

✔ Make photo albums to introduce new places or experiences, such as a new school or a visit to the dentist

✔ Use images to record processes such as bread-making

✔ Provide visual timetables

✔ Use with PowerPoint to create show-and-tell activities

✔ Use Photo Story to create an automatic slide show which can be used to demonstrate a process or record achievement

✔ Use images on interactive whiteboards, adding text and sound as necessary

animation feature. This can also be modified and turned into a game where children select the appropriate preposition which will link them to a slide that asks them to try again or congratulates them and moves them on.

Image technology is an ideal medium for BSL users. By giving them these tools and skills we can let them tell their own stories – and more. They can be expressive and creative and will give us an insight into their view of the world. A video letter is fun but it is also a great resource. It has an intrinsic value, will celebrate Deaf culture and can also be used to teach English. I have a vivid memory recording children's BSL poems about Spring that were both beautiful and moving – but could never be captured on paper. Let's encourage the BSL user to be creative through poetry and drama, develop them through opportunities to use BSL alongside English. With the new generation of cameras and editing software, anyone can gain the skills to capture moments such as these and use them in their teaching.

Brilliant Idea 47

Praise where praise is due

GARETH MOREWOOD **IS** Director of Curriculum Support at Priestnall School, Stockport. He is delighted with the potential of sending good news to parents via their mobile phone.

There's nothing new about sending texts to parents but while many schools use the system to tell parents about school closures or to report infringements of rules, we are trialling a positive 'text home' system.

It is often said that teachers do not have the time to communicate with a large number of parents on a regular basis. But all teachers are aware that positive contact with home can make life better at school and have a positive impact on teaching and learning. The reality is that for all sorts of reasons, phone calls to parents/carers can be very time consuming and school reports are relatively infrequent, just like parent/carer evenings. Using a text messaging system means that teachers can inform parents of progress and achievement far more frequently.

We use Teachers2parents, a fully managed, web-based solution, so all you have to do is to log in to the website and then, with a few simple clicks, you can start sending text messages to hundreds of parents/carers. Each text message is automatically personalised to include the student's name. There is no need to type each message or any part of it.

All the texts are sent immediately and the school can check to see they have been received. This is a very useful facility which will be beneficial if we start to use the system for administrative matters such as reminders of Annual Review meetings. However, our trial was for a specific purpose, to send positive messages home for vulnerable learners so each message is unique.

Parents and carers involved in the scheme so far have been very positive: 'It's an excellent system, I'm really pleased when I get a text,' said one parent, while another said 'It is great to have something positive to talk about as soon as they get home from school.'

Some of the other possible uses of the 'text-home' system are:

1. Reporting test/assessment results.
2. Praising students.
3. Notification of poor behaviour.
4. Reporting punctuality.
5. Reminding of coursework deadlines/follow ups.
6. Homework.
7. Exam dates.
8. Detentions.
9. Incorrect uniform.
10. Equipment.
11. Reminders (parents evening, open evenings, after school classes).

Contacts and information

Teachers2Parents – https://www.teachers2parents.co.uk/
Secondary Contact – http://www.keepkidssafe.co.uk/
Truancy Call – http://www.truancycall.com/http://schoolcomms.com/
Schoolcomms – http://schoolcomms.com/
ParentMail – https://www.parentmail.co.uk/

Brilliant Idea 48

'Come on you lazy lot, let's go adventuring!'

THE LAND OF ME brings together all the best elements of a classic picture story book and ICT. There are six chapters, each with a different theme, which follow the exploits of Buddy Boo the bear, Eric the raccoon and Willow the owl. The adventure unfolds on screen but what happens there is only a small part of the story. Children can make music, construct buildings, choreograph dances and create monsters and more. There are over 100 printable activities, games and puzzles to do away from the computer.

The company Made in Me has worked with Professor John Siraj-Blatchford at Swansea University's Centre for Child Research to make sure that every activity is founded on the most effective techniques for developing language and creativity in young children. Chapter one focuses on shape, size and colour but these themes spawn lots of adjectives too – big, round, purple – so teachers can develop and record receptive language to see how much children understand or use the story as the basis for work on descriptions in literacy. The Land of Me has been used in Early Years settings, primary and in different ways in some special schools and home-based learning. The teaching activities are also geared to support a cross-curricular approach to incorporate science, geography and history as well as creative activities such as art and dance.

Cuckmere House School is a community special school in Seaford, East Sussex for boys aged between five years who need help with behavioural, emotional and social difficulties. Staff used Chapter two, The World Outside, to develop games and activities to support personal, social and emotional wellbeing. Pupils had to choose from a selection of clothing and materials as to the most appropriate for differing weather conditions and environments. They identified each item as it was pulled out of a bag and matched it with the weather and/or terrain it would be used in.

Once all the items were laid out on the floor the teacher would create a 'desert', 'lake' or 'arctic' setting, as in The Land of Me, and the children would then choose an appropriate piece of clothing. Some were not able to do this. As well as looking at weather and climate, they looked at day and night and time zones as these are very relevant to the adventures. Staff found that several pupils needed help understanding with telling the time and using the 24-hour clock.

After working through the story and the related activities, the school realised they needed to refine their personal learning programmes with a greater emphasis on life skills. The Land of Me provided a stimulus and framework for a host of activities as well as being lots of fun.

You could ...

✔ Go onto the Land of Me blog (http://www. madeinme.com/blog/category/free-activities/) and try out the free activities which include matching games and making story dice

✔ Read the case studies on the site which show how it can be used for music, art and craft activities

Contacts and information
http://www.madeinme.com/blog/category/learning/
The work from Cuckmere House School will form part of a new pack of teachers' materials for The Land of Me.

Brilliant Idea 49

Numbed by numbers no longer

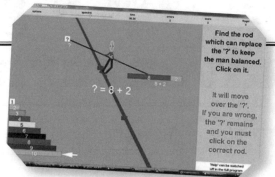

TEACHERS CAN NEVER make enough of their own activities to build number skills, so it is a good idea to have a few ready-made programs in the armoury to help improve familiarity, competence and confidence. Numbershark helps with the understanding of maths by teaching and reinforcing mathematical concepts, using carefully designed games. Students enjoy playing these because they are fun to use while teachers find they help to motivate even the most reluctant of students.

In Tameside they have used Numbershark with Jon, a Year 5 pupil at School Action Plus, working at L1a. He has poor numerical recall but is keen to learn and likes to try new activities. He learns best with repeated activities so using lots of different versions of the same information helps him to learn. They found that if his special needs assistant worked with him she could keep him focused and help him with any reading problems. They decided to concentrate on his multiplication tables as he has some knowledge of basic addition and subtraction but struggles with knowledge of the two times table. Here is a brief account of Jon's progress.

'Jon is very poor at numeracy. We decided to concentrate on multiplication as he struggled to learn the two times table and had little or no knowledge of the five and ten times tables. He was set up with the laptop in three lessons a week, in another lesson he consolidated his knowledge with pen and paper activities using various worksheets and in the fifth lesson he worked in a group completing Springboard 3. We decided to use Numbershark 4 on a one to one basis with the pupil as it offered a wide range of games and activities that would offer him the variety he needs. Using Numbershark we could also offer a structured programme by selecting the objectives that we wanted him to cover. We could keep a record of what areas he excelled at and where he struggled. The programme

Key features

✔ It covers addition, subtraction, multiplication and division

✔ It also covers negatives, percentages, fractions and decimals

✔ The 45 different games are broken down into various categories such as counting, arithmetic concepts or number line and grid

✔ The games use a mixture of spoken voice instructions and different ways of showing the relationships between numbers

✔ Number Shark introduces strategies for problem solving

✔ It encourages children to compete against themselves

✔ Children have their own record of achievement

✔ It works well in the home environment too

also offered a simplified reading scheme that would be easy for him to understand.

'The pupil has made good progress. Over two weeks he has gained a basic knowledge of the two times table and is beginning to make more progress by transferring this to his mental maths (although this is still developing). The variety of games and activities supported his emerging knowledge and helped him gain more confidence. The games were set out very easily and when he got stuck he could use the help area to tell him what to do as it was written in simple language that was at his level. He enjoyed the fact that at the end of each learning activity he was given a game as a reward. We found that the variety of games offered lots of different types of activities so if the pupil did not understand the way it was set out when it was using blocks we could change it to use a pattern or a number square. This way we could personalise the programme even more to the student who quickly realised that he could change it to his preferred method himself.'

Contacts and information

http://www.wordshark.co.uk/numbershark/

Brilliant Idea 50

What happens to hot ice cream?

DATALOGGING FOR CHILDREN has often been overlooked partly because teachers are not sure of how to use the equipment. Using thermometers proved fiddly and the gauge was so small that it was difficult to get an accurate or accessible reading, so for pupils with ADHD this proved to be too much as the results took such a long time to see. LogIT technologies then produced their *LogIT Explorer* datalogger which meant that pupils could easily access a range of measurements.

Danny Nicholson was teaching in a school in Southend and came across two boys who were not able to concentrate for longer than a few minutes on any task and having to share equipment proved too much for them.

'We set up an experiment based on the fact that Southend is the home of one of the most famous ice cream makers in England. Every evening after school the Rossi ice cream van was parked outside the school and sometimes he was there for a long time waiting for the children to come out of school. We decided to find out how long he would have to wait before the ice cream melted and he had to go home.'

Traditionally they would have used a thermometer to measure the temperature but using the LogITs with a temperature probe fitted meant that pupils could go and take the temperature and record on a bar chart what the temperature was every five minutes.

Danny started by taking the temperature of crushed ice using the LogIT and the visualiser. Everyone could see that the temperature was zero degrees. After five minutes the temperature was three degrees and the ice was melting fast.

The question was then asked: 'How could the ice cream man make his ice cream last longer?'

All the children were given various materials to wrap around a plastic cup and the race was on. Bubble wrap, newspaper, cotton wool, plastic, cardboard and materials were all used and every child had their own pot and access to a LogIT to take the temperature every two minutes. Whoever's ice was last to reach three degrees was the winner.

The two boys were engrossed in the process, the posed problem and the ease of use of the LogITs. They were keen to try the experiment again and again with different materials and charted their findings on a bar chart of time taken to thaw. They rushed out to the ice cream man the next day with their findings.

Note: Danny won't tell us which method won – you will just have to find out for yourselves!

Contacts and information

LogIT Explorer – http://www.taglearning.co.uk/

You could ...

✔ Take the temperature of the whole class to see who is the hottest/coldest

✔ Huddle together to see if you get hotter like penguins do in the Antarctic

✔ Use the LogITs to measure noise levels in different parts of the school

✔ Discover which musical instrument made the loudest noise

✔ See who can clap the loudest

✔ Use the LogITs to measure light around the school to find where the best place to grow plants might be

Part 2

Now it's your turn: Brilliant Starters to get you going

Brilliant Starter 1

Using your Smartboard

Using the pens

⮑ Write your name in many colours then move them around to make patterns.

⮑ Use the yellow highlighter to create the name and allow pupils to trace over the top with the creative pens.

⮑ Infinitely clone your name (select the name and go to the drop-down arrow to find the infinite cloner) or turn the words around with the green spot at the top.

⮑ Make them bigger or smaller with the white circle at the bottom right hand corner.

⮑ Brainstorm, asking pupils to write up their suggestions.

⮑ Use the eraser to rub out part of the word to make a basic cloze activity or to investigate symmetry.

⮑ Use the pens to trace around the outside of a shadow or profile cast by the projector and play guess who or guess what!

⮑ Or simply change your selected words to text and use as a word bank.

Using rub and reveal

⮑ To change the colour and width of the pen go to the properties icon and select your colour and pen line style.

⮑ Insert an image or word onto the screen and choose a pen colour the same colour as the background and cover the image with pen. Using the eraser, rub out the layer of pen to reveal the image underneath. This is great for identifying artists, subjects of photos, bugs hidden all over the screen, labels or word hunts!

Using layers

⮑ There are three layers on whiteboard software. Being able to use these means that you can set up fun activities relatively easily. If you put a basket on the notebook page then you can allocate the healthy foods to take on a picnic to the back layer, so they disappear 'into' (behind) the basket. All the unhealthy foods will be on the front layer so will not go into the basket at all.

Manipulating text

⮑ Double click on any piece of text and the editing toolbar appears. Highlight a word and drag it out to get a wordbank or re-highlight the word to colour it. The word could be coloured to accommodate grammatical labels or coloured the same as the background to make a cloze activity. Highlight a phrase to drag it out and make a re-ordering sequencing activity.

Using the extra tools

⮑ Using the camera tool allows you to snap shot any website/picture or even frames from a video.

⮑ The spotlight tool allows you to isolate parts of the screen in a spotlight.

⮑ The blinds tool reveals parts of the screen.

Brilliant Starter 2

Using ActivInspire

Using the pens

○ Write your name in many colours then move them around to make patterns.

○ Use the yellow highlighter to create the name and allow pupils to trace over the top with the creative pens.

○ Duplicate your name (click on the name and go to the object edit icon) or turn the words around with the rotate icon.

○ Make them bigger or smaller with the white circle at the bottom right hand corner.

○ Brainstorm, asking pupils to write up their suggestions.

○ Use the eraser to rub out part of the word to make a basic cloze activity or to investigate symmetry

○ Use the pens to trace around the outside of a shadow or profile cast by the projector and play guess who or guess what!

○ Or simply change your selected words to text and use as a word bank.

Using rub and reveal

○ To change the colour and width of the pen go to pen icon bar and choose from the widths and colours displayed.

○ Insert an image or word onto the screen and choose a pen colour the same colour as the background and cover the image with pen. Using the eraser, rub out the layer of pen to reveal the image underneath. This is great for identifying artists, subjects of photos, bugs hidden all over the screen, labels or word hunts!

○ The magic pen will rub out images on the top layer as well!

Using layers

○ There are three layers on whiteboard software. Being able to use these means that you can set up fun activities relatively easily. If you put a basket on the page then you can allocate the healthy foods to take on a picnic to the back layer, so they disappear 'into' (behind) the basket. All the unhealthy foods will be on the front layer so will not go into the basket at all.

○ To do this, choose the item you want to go behind the basket, click on the image and select 'Send to back' from the icon bar displayed. It's that easy!

○ Using this technique you can put prime numbers in a box, rhyming words into a bowl or bring treasure out of a treasure chest!

Manipulating text

⮑ Double click on any piece of text and the editing toolbar appears. Highlight a word and drag it out to get a wordbank or re-highlight the word to colour it. The word could be coloured to accommodate grammatical labels or coloured the same as the background to make a cloze activity. Highlight a phrase to drag it out and make a re-ordering sequencing activity. The fill bucket will colour your words when you click on them!

Using the extra tools

⮑ The tools icon opens a treasure chest of fantastic tools to use on your screen.

⮑ The revealer obscures a part of the screen allowing you to reveal the part that you want examined.

⮑ The camera takes a picture of a small area of a website or video which will then pop straight onto the page. These images can then be stored under the 'My Content' section of the Gallery.

Brilliant Starter 3

Using symbol software

Communicate in Print is a symbol software from Widgit. Symbols are a fantastic way to convey the meaning of language supported by visual imagery. Here are some ways to use this software.

- ⮑ Use it to symbolise a piece of text to aid comprehension and independence when reading.
- ⮑ Open the software.
- ⮑ Choose the top icon (an owl with no red border).
- ⮑ Open up the text box on your page and type.
- ⮑ Symbols will appear above your text.
- ⮑ Three keys on your keyboard will tailor the symbols to your needs.
- ⮑ F9 will toggle through all the available symbols.
- ⮑ F10 will delete symbols for frequently occurring words that the pupil already knows so leaving a less cluttered page.
- ⮑ F11 will delete the text underneath the symbol to allow you to personalise the symbol ... press the right arrow key to add the symbol/text association to be saved onto your computer.

Create a table for a word grid or game

- ⮑ Make a single cell with the second icon down (the owl with a red frame around it).
- ⮑ Then go to Frames and Pictures on the top menu bar and choose Make a table.
- ⮑ You can choose how many cells across and down.
- ⮑ Type into the cells.

Insert a picture or photo from Widgits categories

- ⮑ Choose the yellow folder icon and select a category from the panel on the right.
- ⮑ Click on your selected picture and click on the page.

Insert your own picture from your computer

⮑ Click on the Picture A tab at the bottom of the pictures panel. This will open all the files you have in My Pictures on your computer.

⮑ If the pictures are somewhere else (i.e. your network) click on the drop-down arrow at the top of the pictures panel to select the location of your saved files.

⮑ You can use these pictures above any text on your page by clicking the picture and clicking the word.

Add a speech bubble to a picture to make a poster or comic book

⮑ Click on the speech bubble icon on the left hand panel.

⮑ Select the kind of speech bubble and direction on the right hand panel and expand an area on your page by clicking and dragging a rectangle on your page.

⮑ Type straight into the speech bubble.

Widgit software has a comprehensive manual under the Help drop-down menu at the top of the window.

Brilliant Starter 4

Using your camera

➲ Your camera should have a download lead that plugs into the camera via a small plug and then into your computer or laptop via a normal USB plug.

➲ The camera needs to be switched to download on the dial or sliding switch that selects whether you will be using still images or video. This symbol usually looks like a rectangle with an arrow pointing away from it (but this can vary from camera to camera).

➲ As soon as the camera is connected in this way, and is switched on, a window will appear asking you what you would like to do with the pictures.

➲ Select what you want to do with the pictures!

➲ Do remember which folder you have downloaded your pictures to… many is the time that I have spent trying to discover where I have downloaded my pictures!

➲ Now is the time to go onto a website such as www.bighugelabs.com to do fun stuff with your photos or to go to the Photo Story 3 download site to get some free presentation software.

Your photos can now be used in your interactive whiteboard software, wordprocessing software or downloaded onto digital photoframes to scroll through selections of photos automatically.

Brilliant Starter 5

Using sound

There is an excellent, simple to use free software download (http://audacity.sourceforge.net/) which can be used to record sounds and then edit them and add effects.

⊃ Connect your microphone and use record, stop and play buttons to hear your work. The audio track appears as you record.

⊃ If you record further then a second audio track appears underneath. Both tracks are then played at once. Clicking Mute prevents a track being played. Clicking Solo ensures only the selected track is played.

⊃ Once audio tracks are recorded you can use the Select tool to select a piece and use the Edit menu to cut or copy sounds. They can be combined onto one track or different tracks can be used for different types of sounds.

⊃ To hear part of a track select it and then click Play. Click on Edit and then Silence to insert a silence. Edit split takes the highlighted section out and moves it onto a new track leaving a rest in its place.

⊃ To use effects highlight your piece of sound and then click on Effects and select from the drop-down options. Effects work cumulatively, one on top of the other until you turn them off. You can use undo as many times as you need to when using effects.

Brilliant Starter 6

Using Easi-Speak microphones

- ⮕ Switch on the on/off switch at the side of the microphone to 'on'.

- ⮕ Press and release the red record button. The LED will go red meaning you are recording (if it doesn't, press it again!).

- ⮕ Press and release the red record button to stop recording.

- ⮕ Press the green button to play your recording.

- ⮕ To play different tracks, press play (green button) then forward or back on the yellow buttons (just above the on/off switch).

- ⮕ The middle yellow button (*) toggles between MP3 recordings and WAV files.

To download a file

- ⮕ Insert the usb into your computer (pull off the end of the microphone).

- ⮕ Navigate to the files. Go to Removable disk/mic rec file and find your file from there.

- ⮕ This is the easiest way to delete files (right mouse click on the file and choose Delete).

- ⮕ To download into Audacity:

  - ⮕ Open Audacity. Go to File > Open and navigate to the file.

  - ⮕ Save as normal.

Brilliant Starter 7

Inserting sound files into PowerPoint, Notebook or ActivInspire

To insert into PowerPoint

➲ Highlight the word and right click on it or the picture that you wish to link to a sound file.

➲ From the drop-down menu choose action settings.

➲ Go to the bottom where it says play sound and scroll down to the option that says 'other'. Navigate to the place where you have saved the sound effect that you want.

And Smart Notebook

➲ Click on the image or word, select Sound from the drop-down menu.

➲ Navigate to the required sound.

And ActivInspire

➲ Open a flipchart and ensure you are in design mode (F2). Click on an image and go to Insert link to file and choose your sound file.

➲ The next screen asks for the details and it is a good idea to embed the sound into the flipchart.

➲ OK will confirm this request.

➲ Press F2 to go back to presenting mode and your image will play the requested file.

Inserting hyperlinks into PowerPoint, Notebook or ActivInspire

To insert into PowerPoint

➲ Highlight the word or picture and right click on it.

➲ From the drop-down menu choose Hyperlink.

➲ Choose the file and location that you want to link to (don't forget you can link to other pages in your presentation to make a non-linear book).

And Smart Notebook

➲ Click on the image or word, select Link from the drop-down menu.

➲ Navigate to the required page or file.

And ActivInspire

➲ Open a flipchart and ensure you are in design mode (F2). Click on an image and go to Insert link to file and choose your file.

➲ The next screen asks for the details and it is a good idea to embed the file into the flipchart if it is an external file.

➲ OK will confirm this request.

➲ Press F2 to go back to presenting mode and your image will link to the requested file.

Brilliant Starter 9

Inserting custom animation into PowerPoint

PowerPoint is a much used, much loathed program, seen in every course attended by teachers. But, by putting in custom animation, it is transformed into a fun format for pupils to write and enjoy their own stories.

◯ Putting in custom animation:

　　◯ Insert a picture (Insert, Picture, Clipart/From File).

　　◯ Click on it so that small circular placeholders appear.

　　◯ Go to Custom animation (in the Slide show drop-down menu or on the View ribbon).

　　◯ Go to Add Effect. You will discover all kinds of ways that your image can enter or exit the page.

　　◯ To add a free moving animation go to Motion paths and draw custom path.

Using Word

Choosing the best font

- The fonts you use are really important. Choose an illegible curly font and the task of reading the text becomes much harder even though it might look prettier! The default is Times New Roman but you can set your own default.

- Go to Format > Font and choose the style, size and colour from the window that opens.

- Click on default at the bottom left hand corner and your computer will be set to your preferred default.

Using tables

- Click on the tables icon on the toolbar or ribbon and click on the first cell and extend your mouse click diagonally to the right until you have included as many rows and columns as you need.

- To insert a picture or text just click inside the cell and insert the picture.

- To alter the first column whilst leaving the other columns of equal width, hold down Ctrl whilst moving the cell line.

- The Tables toolbar will allow you to colour, merge and filter your table.

Using Autoshapes

- The Autoshapes can be accessed via the drawing toolbar. There are lots of certificates, speech bubbles as well as a host of fun shapes to use in posters. To write inside any of the shapes, right mouse click and select Add text.

Using bullets and borders

- Bullets, especially if they are picture bullets, are a great way of breaking up big blocks of text. Click on the bullet icon, go to Format on the drop-down menu and choose Bullets and numbering.

- Click on Customize and Character and then choose Webdings or Wingdings from the drop-down menu. A whole range of pictures and symbols should appear. Choose one and click on OK.

- Borders just make documents look more appealing! Click on Format in the drop-down menu, choose Borders and shading, Page borders and then look for the Art drop-down menu at the bottom of the window. There are lots of great borders to choose from.

Importing and watermarking images

➲ Importing images is very straightforward. Click on Insert and then choose Pictures > From File and navigate to your own picture (or choose Clip art and type in the subject for a choice of clip art images).

➲ When the image goes into your document a toolbar appears which allows you to 'wrap' the image, i.e. move it about or watermark the image into the back of your document so that you can type over it.

➲ When the image goes into your document there is a solid line around it. To release the image go to the picture of a dog and select one of the options.

➲ To watermark an image into the background of your document go to the two tubes icon and select Washout.

Choosing a suitable spelling program

There are lots of programs on the market to help with phonics and letter blends and to help children develop an eye and an ear for spelling. Here are some guidelines to help you choose the ones which will be effective with your learners.

Is the display clear?

⮑ For learners who have problems with information processing, a cluttered screen with distracting colours and movement can hinder understanding.

Does it feature anagrams?

⮑ For learners with dyslexia, this is not a good idea.

Can the speed of presentation and response be altered?

⮑ A program that flashes information onto the screen too quickly or requires a reaction beyond the capabilities of the learner will encourage guessing instead of a considered response; a program that moves too slowly will result in poor concentration. A long introduction is useful first time round, but becomes boring once you know it too well.

Can the length of the game be altered?

⮑ A good game will allow the teacher to decide the number of goes or the success rate to be achieved for successful completion.

Can the sound level be altered?

⮑ A nasty noise that broadcasts the fact that you have made an error is not helpful for some learners.

Does the program save the settings?

⮑ It is a boon in a busy schedule if next time you come to the program, you can continue with the same options.

Does the program encourage the learner to work independently?

⮑ Is the task clear? Will the learner need to read on-screen instructions in order to tackle the required task? Are essential instructions spoken and/or can they be read by a screen reader if needed?

⮑ The teacher chose a program for Hugh, with target words within his reading level. The 'carrier language', which is the on-screen instructions and sentences surrounding the target words, were too advanced, leaving Hugh unable to work independently.

Can word lists be edited?

➲ A good program will allow the teacher to enter word lists designed to support the learner's learning and to include subject specific vocabulary.

What happens when the learner makes a mistake?

➲ There is nothing worse than getting caught in a loop where the software will not continue unless you get the answer right but provides no help if you get it wrong.

Does it use rewards and penalties?

➲ James, Year 6, loved playing a spelling game where if he got the word wrong, a little man would appear on the screen, pick up the word, screw it up and throw it into a dustbin. Unfortunately, James found it more fun to get the word wrong! Here the penalties were more attractive than the rewards and got in the way of learning.

Are there home user versions of the program?

➲ Parents often appreciate being involved and if there is a home version of the program it can provide a focus for targeted work. These programs provide structure and often have a fun competitive element which is a boon when it comes to homework.

Brilliant Starter 12

Using Clicker 5

- ➲ Open the program and choose a grid to open in the examples folder.

- ➲ Hold down Shift and left click in a cell. You can now change the word in that cell to customise any resource to fit your pupil.

- ➲ Right click on any cell to hear it read to you.

- ➲ Left click on any cell to send the word to a writing window or make a choice in the labelling activities.

- ➲ To change any image go to the Edit drop-down menu and select Edit mode.

- ➲ Choose the picture icon and either make a selection from the Crick picture library to drag and drop into your grid or go to Computer and navigate to where your pictures are stored and drag them on.

- ➲ To make your own grid, go to the home screen (click on the house icon) and choose Create new grid set.

- ➲ A choice of formats opens up and you will need to open (by clicking on them) a number of folders before getting to the final choice.

- ➲ Click on Create and the template will open up.

- ➲ Shift-click to add a word or choose a lecture as before.

- ➲ There is an immense amount of free resources to download from www.learninggrids.com. You need to register but it is all free.

- ➲ Once downloaded you can adapt the grids as detailed above.

Brilliant Starter 13

Using GarageBand

➡ Open GarageBand and make sure New Project and Piano are selected or the podcast icon if you wish to record your voice.

➡ Click on Choose and select a destination and title for your track and click Create.

➡ In the window that opens choose a category of sound file from the right hand window and a selection of clips will appear under the category panel.

➡ Drag a clip onto your editing window (in the middle of the screen) and drop it in the correct position.

➡ Try dragging another sound file onto the track and you will find it drops in underneath the previous one.

➡ To move the tracks just click and drag.

➡ To make one track fade in or out or just become quieter click on the small drop-down arrow on the left-hand side of the track (it is in a small toolbar).

➡ An editing track appears and if you click underneath your track on the line a dot will appear. Click again a bit further along and you will be able to drag the line up or down to alter the volume.

➡ To listen to your track click on the space bar on your keyboard.

➡ The return key on your keyboard returns the playhead line to the beginning of your composition.

➡ To save your song, click on Share from the toolbar at the top of your screen, click on Export and choose a destination.

➡ Click on Save to complete your first composition using GarageBand.

Brilliant Starter 14

Using I Can Animate

➲ Connect a camera to your computer.

➲ Click on Camera to start capturing your movie.

➲ To capture a frame, click on the Capture button. You can also use the keyboard shortcut Ctrl + Enter or the number 1.

➲ Use the numbers 2 to 9 to capture that number of frames if you want the action to pause for a small time. Three is usually a good choice and gives a smoother result.

➲ Note: Click in the Frames View or in the Preview Area before using the numbers 1 to 9 to capture a frame or frames.

➲ When you have captured a frame, a small thumbnail will appear in the Frames View at the bottom of the main window.

➲ Make some small appropriate changes to the items you are animating and capture another frame.

➲ Continue to do this until you have finished the action you wish to create. You should also regularly save your work.

➲ To save your work, choose File > Save from the menu bar. A dialogue box will open asking you to choose a location and a file name for your project.

➲ Click on the Play button to play back your sequence of frames.

➲ Choose File > Export from the menu bar.

Brilliant Starter 15
Using I Can Present

⮑ Set up a green screen against a wall with even light falling onto it.

⮑ Connect a camera to your computer if your computer doesn't have an in-built camera.

⮑ Connect a microphone if your computer doesn't have an in-built microphone.

⮑ Open the software and click on Backgrounds.

⮑ From this menu choose a suitable photo background. If there are no suitable ones in the categories listed, click on Import and browse for your own photo or image saved onto your computer.

⮑ When you have found a suitable photo click on Choose.

⮑ Then type in any text you wish to appear on the autocue in the text box below the picture.

⮑ Click on Recording studio.

⮑ You may need to select the camera you have connected by clicking on the Video input drop-down menu.

⮑ You may need to choose a microphone from the Audio input drop-down menu.

⮑ Now the magic happens! All the green background will have become transparent and your picture will appear behind the person sitting in front of the camera.

⮑ When you click on the red camera button you will get a 5-second countdown and the recording will start.

⮑ Click on the grey camera button to finish.

⮑ Your video will immediately play back the recording.

⮑ Click on Export to export your video and choose a suitable format and destination.

⮑ Your video will then be ready to play independently from the program.

Using iMovie

○ Connect the digital video camcorder to the computer with the firewire cord.

○ Turn on camcorder.

○ Select iMovie program.

○ Double click on the iMovie folder, then the iMovie icon.

○ Make sure your machine is set on Thousands of Colours on the control strip.

○ Click on New Project.

○ Title your movie and click on Create.

Recording live

○ Press Play on the camcorder and your video should be displayed on the LCD display screen on the camcorder and the computer.

Importing digital video into a movie

○ Make sure the Mode Switch is set to Camera mode

or

○ Use the Camera playback controls to view the tape in the iMovie screen on the computer.

○ Click the Play button. When the iMovie monitor displays the scene you want to use, click the Import button to begin importing.

○ To stop importing, click the Import button again.

○ Select a clip, drag it down to the Timeline at the bottom and use play controls underneath to review clip.

Splitting video clips

○ Click on the clip to select it.

○ Move the playhead (red line) to where you want to split it.

○ Choose Split Video Clip at Playhead from the Edit menu.

○ If you want to remove part of the clip, click on it to select it, and click on Delete.

Adding and editing titles

➲ Select a title style from the list in the middle of the Titles panel.

➲ To speed up or slow down the titling effect, adjust the speed and/or pause sliders.

➲ If a title scrolls, you can change the direction it scrolls by clicking on the arrows on the direction button.

➲ Drag the title from the list in the middle of the Titles panel to the clip viewer.

➲ If you want the title to appear over a clip, place it before that clip. A title icon appears between the clips, and a small progress bar appears under it.

Adding scene transitions

➲ Transitions smooth the cuts between scenes (clips).

➲ Click the Transitions button (T).

➲ Select a transition in the Transitions panel.

➲ Drag the transition from the Transitions panel to the desired location in the timeline viewer.

Adding music: to record audio CD music into your movie

➲ Click the Audio button.

➲ Insert the audio CD into your computer's CD-ROM drive.

➲ If the CD automatically starts playing through your computer's speaker, stop it by clicking the Play button on the Audio panel.

Select a track in the Audio panel and do one of the following:

➲ Drag the audio CD track from the panel to audio track 1 or 2 in the timeline viewer.

➲ Click the Record Music button on the Audio panel to start recording music into your movie. To end recording, click the Stop button.

Extracting audio from a video clip

➲ If a video clip already contains audio when you import it, you can remove it from the clip.

➲ In the timeline viewer, select the video clip that contains the audio you want to extract.

➲ Choose Extract Audio from Advanced on the menu bar. The extracted audio appears in audio track 1.

➲ When you extract audio, you copy (not remove) it from the video clip.

➲ However, iMovie turns the volume of the video clip all the way down when you extract the audio, so you won't hear the audio in the original video clip anymore.

➲ When you have finished creating your iMovie, go to File > Export Movie > Export.

➲ You can then choose how to export the file and where to save it.

Using Movie Maker

⊃ Connect a video camera to your computer and Open the software.

⊃ In the Movie Tasks pane, under Capture Video, click Capture from video device.

⊃ On the Video Capture Device page, in Available devices, click your camera, then Next.

⊃ Enter a file name for your captured video and choose Best quality for playback on my computer as a setting.

⊃ Click Next.

⊃ Click Start Capture and press play on your camera. Movie Maker will begin transferring video to your computer.

⊃ Your clips will be in the Collection pane. Double click on a clip to play it in the preview window. Drag the clips you want to use onto the storyboard at the bottom of the screen.

⊃ To rearrange your clips on the storyboard, just drag and drop them to a different location.

⊃ You can edit your clips to make sure you keep only the footage you want.

⊃ Switch from storyboard to timeline view (click Show Timeline, just above the storyboard).

⊃ Click the clip you want to edit; you will see small black arrows at each end of the clip, and a blue timeline marker:

   ⊃ If you want to cut footage from the beginning of the clip, click on the left hand arrow and drag it slowly to the right until you reach the point you want – you will be able to see where you are in the preview window.

   ⊃ Audio tracks can be added to your movie. First, in Capture Video in the Tasks Menu, click Import audio or music. Browse your way to where your audio/music is stored, and select the files you want to use. They will appear as part of your collection.

   ⊃ Drop in the clip and trim to fit as before.

   ⊃ Right clicking on the Audio/Music track will give a menu which allows you to modify your added audio. Fade In and Fade Out are particularly useful (they help to make transitions smoother). You can do the same with the audio track which is attached to your video clip – it's sometimes useful to mute this if you don't need the soundtrack you have recorded.

   ⊃ You can change the way one clip leads into the next by adding video transitions.

⊃ In the Movie Tasks pane, under Edit Movie, click View video transitions. Select the transition effect you would like, and drag it to the transition cell between the two clips you are working on.

⊃ Finally, you can add titles, captions and credits to your film. In the Movie Tasks pane, under Edit Movie, click Make titles or credits. This gives you the option of creating a title as an opening sequence to your film, credits to go at the end, or captions before/on/after any clip. Simply type text in the box, choose your font, background colour and title animation, and click 'Done, add title to movie' when you have finished.

Using Photo Story 3

- ⊃ Download Photo Story 3 from the Microsoft website.

- ⊃ Select Begin a new story. Other options are to edit or play a story.

- ⊃ Click on Import pictures to browse for images you want to use.

- ⊃ The imported pictures appear on a track underneath and can be re-ordered by clicking on the picture and then arrows.

- ⊃ Clicking on effect below a picture that is being displayed enables you to select from a range of picture effects.

- ⊃ Click Next.

- ⊃ Click on each picture in turn and add labels by typing into the text box. Text options are available above this to change font and position text.

- ⊃ Use the red record button to record your narration to the images. Use the preview button to watch your photo story.

- ⊃ Click Next.

- ⊃ Use the customise motion button to set the transition between pictures and the start and end points of any motion by dragging the handles.

- ⊃ Add background music by clicking on Select music to browse for any music on your computer.

- ⊃ The create music button allows you to select from options to create your own music.

- ⊃ Save your story allows you to select from a number of save options depending on what you want to use the Photo Story for. Make sure you also save your work as a project as you may want to edit and reuse it later.

- ⊃ Click on Next, browse to a place to save your movie file and save. This will take a few moments to save all aspects of your movie.

Brilliant starter to making comics with Comic Life or Big Huge Labs.

Brilliant Starter 19

Creating a comic with Comic Life

- Select a template for your new page or you can create your own layout by dragging panels anywhere you want them.

- Add digital images from your library, other disks or a connected digital camera. You can drag and drop images into the Comic life interface (from your library or any connected disk), or you can drag items directly from the camera's DCIM file into Comic Life.

- Dragging an image onto a panel will put the image into the panel and crop it so the shortest dimension of the image matches the shortest dimension of the panel. You can adjust the panel size/shape separately from the image's size.

- Select a style/filter for digital images. You can leave your images in their unfiltered state, but Comic Life's built-in filters and styles give you some very cool control over how 'comicy' your comic looks. If you don't like the pre-defined styles, you can enter your own filter settings to get that perfect look.

- Don't overlook the fact that you can draw your own images (on the computer, or on paper and scan them in) and then include them in your comic once they are in a digital format.

- Add text containers and text. Just like almost everything else in Comic Life, adding text is a simple drag and drop process. The text containers at the bottom of the window provide you with different text presentations.

- Drag a container into your page and enter your text. If you have a balloon selected, you can drag the tail to associate the speech or thought with a particular character in an image. Additional tails can be added for more than one speaker at a time.

- Other text containers have options for styles and effects to enhance the text. The controls allow you to stretch, scale, skew, colorise, outline, shade and too many other options to list. The pre-defined options are numerous and individual controls let you take them further.

- Save (frequently) and export to your format of choice. The HTML export creates an interface that allows users to 'flip' through your comic page-by-page.

- Big Huge Labs (www.bighugelabs.com) has a free Captioner that enables you to quickly make a comic-style poster from your own digital images.

- These have 'wows' and 'pows' to add as well.

- This free program is great for posters, labels and jokes.

Brilliant Starter 20

Making printable books with Publisher

- Open Publisher.

- Start with making a choice from the Publications to Print choice. These have ready made templates that will accommodate most needs. Brochure or Catalog would suit books best.

- To add or change the pictures, text or WordArt go to View, Toolbars and choose Objects. This will give you a toolbar with more options to work with.

- Add text – click the Text box icon on the toolbar, then click and drag on your page.

- Add WordArt – click the WordArt icon on the toolbar, type your text, then position and re-size your WordArt.

- Add clip art – click the Clip art icon on the toolbar, type in a search term (right hand side of the screen), then click your chosen clip and position it on your slide.

- Add an AutoShape – click the Autoshapes icon on the toolbar, choose your shape, then click and drag to place your shape on your slide. Change colours using the fill and line tools on the formatting toolbar.

To make a printable book

- Click on Publications to Print.

- Choose Catalog (American spelling!)

- Select your favourite design.

- Use the Objects toolbar to replace the picture....click on the picture icon, draw a frame around the area to put the picture in, select either ClipArt or Picture from File and choose a picture. Resize as appropriate.

- In the panel on the left hand side you can choose different colour or font styles.

- In that same panel you can choose the design or different picture for each page.

This will make a folded book...it's important to work out which page occurs next in the correct order!!

The last word...

This book is all about using ICT to enrich the lives of those with mild to moderate difficulties and, by giving you 50 great ways to use ICT in an imaginative way we hope we have done that.

Our thanks go to all those imaginative and creative teachers and software developers who have identified a difficulty and addressed it by the innovative use of ICT and especially the people who have contributed their experiences for this book. We have loved putting it together and have enjoyed finding out how others have used the technology so enthusiastically.

Let's leave you with a few comments from teachers and pupils who have used the ideas in this book and used ICT as a tool to create rich learning experiences.

'I can't wait to use sound with the children.' Liz Hall, SCITT student, Billericay SCITT

'This is just like magic! Can we do it again please?' Pupil, Pioneer School, Basildon

'We have created some 'magic paper'. Their name is hidden on the board but it is written in the same colour as the background so it is invisible until they drag a square of a different colour over it. Then their name magically appears and they can look and see how it is spelt and have another go.' Louise Warton, teaching assistant

'We want to ensure that our learners are as independent as possible and we focus a lot on finding strategies that work for individuals.' Steve Harris, Richard Lander School

'Charlie is now learning to learn and enjoying becoming a reader.' Kate Ruddle, Great Heath Primary School

---

What can I use?

Commercial resources:
Cobalt Flux – http://www.fitnessgaming.co.uk/
The Cyber Coach – http://www.cyber-coach.co.uk/
Key Skills Dance Mat – http://www.tts-group.co.uk/ search for dance mat

---

Afterword: making it happen – Lorraine Petersen

Training for teachers is essential or all the money spent on technology will be wasted. We have many effective, experienced special needs co-ordinators (SENCOs) in our schools today, but over half are due to retire in the next five years so any programme needs to be ongoing. The role of the SENCO is central. They need the time and resources to manage the SEN provision, to co-ordinate the assessment of pupils and to ensure that the school can meet individual needs.

Teachers often ask how can we motivate learners who have rejected the core curriculum? They ask questions such as, 'I have an autistic child in my classroom and he is completely disengaged. What can I do?' Many of the training programs see technology as a conduit to the standard curriculum rather than as a subject in its own right. For children with special needs, technology may be the only route into education. It might provide them with access to speech and language, to writing and recording or inspire them with new ways to connect with education. My gripe is that so many schools ban phones and PSPs. Yet there is evidence that these are the very tools needed for some children. It comes back to teaching and leadership and an understanding of what is needed.

I have gone into primary schools which spent thousands of pounds of e-Learning credits but there is little evidence of technology until you open the cupboards and boxes fall out. There is also the issue of ageing technology. For example, in many authorities the interactive whiteboards and projectors were all installed during the same period and they are all coming to the end of their shelf life at the same time, just when budgets are under pressure. Maintenance may not be a priority so once equipment is old, goes out of fashion or needs repairing it goes back in the cupboard. Sometimes it just needs a minor adjustment or to be used in a slightly different way and it can be used to benefit groups of children in the school. But how can you improve special needs practice if teachers don't know what's out there or how to use it? How do you provide progression for a child who has grown out of a piece of technology? Parents need to feel confident that all teachers are equipped with the necessary knowledge to support their child and the answer to this lies in effective training.

Whatever resources you put into schools you need to back it up with training. Many teachers trained a long time ago when technology was not as advanced or available as it is now. Older teachers may not be ICT savvy and my concern is that if we lose the expertise and support currently offered by Local Authority personnel, there will be no intermediary to advise and help schools in their purchasing decisions. There is a danger that companies will jump on the bandwagon and sell schools equipment that they don't need and which will not meet the needs of children with special needs.

In the past we have had some very successful training programs. While some felt there was a post code lottery and that provision was inconsistent, it did offer some good models for Continual Professional Development (CPD) for individuals and for whole-school staff development. Now there are new challenges. In April the new Equality Duty means that schools must provide aids and support for those children who need them. How many schools are confident they can meet their legal requirements? Special schools need to offer their expertise to other schools in their area. The BSF model of a hub of schools with a special school at the core was a very creative and effective model and could provide a cost effective way of sharing knowledge and good practice.

So what can a school do?

➲ Audit your resources: what have you got and, most importantly, does it work?

➲ Have your staff been trained? What sort of training have they had and how recent?

➲ What are the needs of the students?

➲ Match up the teacher skills and pupil needs and decide where the gaps are.

➲ Develop a strategic plan of what you need to buy in and decide priorities.

➲ Identify expertise in your local area and find ways of tapping into it. Schools need to work together instead of competing.

Lorraine Petersen is Chief Executive of NASEN (National Association for Special Educational Needs).

About the authors

Sal McKeown

These days I earn my living through consultancy and writing, but I taught in schools and colleges for many years and worked with students who had many and varied learning needs from sensory disabilities to mental health issues and autism. My special area of interest is dyslexia although I won the 2006 Journalist of the Year Award for responsible reporting about epilepsy. My 'wow' moment with technology came early on when I worked in adult literacy with people who had severe learning difficulties. Most of this group could only spell a few words and even those were more often wrong than right. We offered work placements to trainee teachers of office skills who ran lunchtime touch-typing classes. Several of the students had a go and I noticed that their spelling improved quite dramatically. They had absorbed patterns through their fingertips and would sit in class, a pen in one hand, while the other hand marked out shapes on the table. '"Was" is a triangle,' said Sheila, 'and "were" is three steps forward and one back.' This was kinaesthetic learning with a difference and quite a change from drills and skills spelling programs which were our only strategy at that time. I have been a fan of technology and compensatory strategies ever since. They reach parts of the brain that other teaching will never touch.

➲ For further information see http://www.sallymckeown.co.uk

Angie McGlashon

I have worked in the area of ICT and SEN since joining the special needs support service in Essex in 1983. Before that I had been a primary school teacher for many years, but joining the team enabled me to identify what a fantastic tool we now had to inspire, encourage and enable children with a variety of difficulties to access the curriculum. I always liken it to a jigsaw puzzle; there was the curriculum and there was a struggling pupil and now there was a variety of access and imaginative programs to enable the child to bridge the gap. I have since worked for a variety of organisations and companies including Widgit software where the power of using images, symbols and visual technologies opened up a whole new means of communication for those who struggled with the conventional text-based approaches. Meeting Sal and sharing her copious knowledge further inspired me to find ways of 'bending' technologies to suit a variety of special needs. I think we are so fortunate to live in a world where people can choose from a range of approaches to participate in the world on an equal level. This book illustrates just how many fantastic ways teachers, carers and people with difficulties can participate in accessing the world around them and enjoy life. I have loved investigating the many new and emerging technologies around at the moment and cannot wait to see what the creative brains of software and hardware companies have to offer us in the future.

➲ For further information see http://edit-training.co.uk/

Index